Bertalan Szemere

Civilization In Hungary

Bertalan Szemere

Civilization In Hungary

ISBN/EAN: 9783741151279

Manufactured in Europe, USA, Canada, Australia, Japa

Cover: Foto ©ninafisch / pixelio.de

Manufactured and distributed by brebook publishing software (www.brebook.com)

Bertalan Szemere

Civilization In Hungary

CIVILIZATION IN HUNGARY:

SEVEN ANSWERS TO THE SEVEN LETTERS

ADDRESSED BY

M. BARTH. DE SZEMERE,

LATE MINISTER OF THE INTERIOR IN HUNGARY,

TO

RICHARD COBDEN, ESQ., M.P. FOR ROCHDALE.

BY

AN HUNGARIAN

Prima est historiæ lex, ne quid *falsi* dicere audeat: deinde, ne quid *veri* non audeat!—M. T. CICERO.

LONDON:
TRÜBNER & CO., 60, PATERNOSTER ROW.

MDCCCLX.

[*The right of translation is reserved by the Author.*]

STEPHEN AUSTIN, PRINTER, HERTFORD.

PREFACE.

There is hardly any country about which so many false ideas are propagated as Hungary; and M. Barth. de Szemere has considerably increased these false ideas, by publishing recently seven letters upon Hungary,[*] which he has addressed to Mr. Cobden, M.P. These letters are full of assertions calculated to confirm certain prejudiced opinions which prevail concerning his country. Hungary certainly occupies an important position in the Austrian dominions, but by no means such an important one as is generally supposed; for it can only occasion negative injury, it cannot effect anything positive in the present complication of Eastern politics, especially if Magyar views were carried out.

[*] "Hungary, from 1848 to 1860," by Barth. de Szemere. London: R. Bentley, 1860.

Szemere is a man of talent and possesses a great many good ideas; he was very active as a philanthropist in introducing reforms in the management of the prisons of his native country, and was also known in the Hungarian literature as the author of some very interesting travels. He was the only Magyar republican in the government of 1848, and energetically resisted the dreams of establishing a Kossuth dynasty, which were supposed to hover before the ambitious vision of M., but more particularly Madame, Kossuth; and this was the cause of the enmity which broke out in exile between the late governor of Hungary and his prime minister.

In consequence of this strife, Szemere wrote a book against Kossuth, published by Campe, in Hamburg, in which he ascribes the failure of the political movement in 1848-49 solely to Kossuth's incapability and want of character in general, and of diplomatic talent in particular. During the Revolution, Szemere seemed to stand forward as the representative of the principles which I have warmly advocated in the following pages, in opposition to those of the exclusive Magyars. To his honour be it said that he, as Minister of the Interior, had the courage to translate all official despatches and circulars sent to the authorities of the different nationalities, into their respective languages, and consequently had to endure a great deal from the ultra-national press. He even went further than this, for he employed two Jews in his office as ministerial officials, and this he graciously signified, when giving a list of his officials, by attaching an asterisk to their names, with the remark "This is a Jew."

I was, therefore, much surprised, on reading M. de Szemere's work, to find him advocating the interests of the exclusive Magyars, and I determined to try and place these interests in their true light, according to modern ideas of State-policy based upon the writings of the highest authorities in England, Germany, and France, viz., Herder, Kant, Hegel, Hormayer, Adam Smith, Buckle, Mill, Blanqui, etc. I have endeavoured to throw light upon the past, present, and future of Hungary by historical facts, rather than by hypothetical assertions; these historical facts I have taken principally from Magyar, liberal, and anti-Austrian historians, such as Fessler, Kubinyi, Graig, Verböczi, Katona, Pray, Széchényi, etc. I leave the just and impartial English Press,—which is accustomed to listen calmly to both sides of a question, and give judgment in favour only of right reasoning, and conclusions drawn by means of induction,—to form for themselves a just opinion of the relative positions of Hungary and Austria. The English Press will then fulfil a high mission, by influencing the public opinion of England, as well as that of Hungary and Austria, encouraging the government of the latter country to continue the liberal reform commenced on the 19th of April; and, at the same time, it will oblige the Magyars to renounce all hopes of exclusive dominion based upon their old constitution, and the supremacy of their nationality.

An intellectual critic, in the *Saturday Review*,* remarks, Szemere has made the great

* See *Saturday Review*, No. 250, Vol. 9, p. 376.

historical mistake of looking "on the events of 1848-49 as isolated from all that had gone before." I have endeavoured to rectify this historical mistake. It was my wish to show the deplorable effects of those causes which brought Hungary into its present condition, to all those who will not acknowledge the great truth in the development of the life of a nation, that the present is but the legitimate child of the past.

Instead of a Preface, M. de Szemere gives us a statistical introduction, to prove to us that the Magyars are numerically superior to the other nationalities. I have endeavoured to show where he was incorrect, and will now add a few statistical remarks, which will clearly confirm my statement, that Germanism alone is the centre of all commercial, industrial, and intellectual power in Austria.

There are about 7642 manufactories in the Austrian empire; 4124 of which are in the hands of Germans, and are worked with 235 steam machines of 5470 horse-power. Two millions and a half of the Austrian population belong to the industrial classes, one million and a half of which are Germans; the other million consists of people from the fifteen different nationalities. In 1841 the value of the productions of the larger manufactories exceeded 593,418,000fl., that of the smaller manufactories 201,599,000 fl. in all 795,017,000 fl. Hungary, Croatia, and Dalmatia, however, are not included in these calculations, because their manufactories are too insignificant. The cotton manufactories, which are most numerous in Lower Austria and Bohemia, there being hardly any in Hungary, keep more than 90,000 looms and 1,268,000 spinning wheels constantly at work. In 1841 there were about 412 wool manufactories in Moravia, Austria, and Bohemia, and the value of their productions amounted to about 75,845,000 fl. There are 8,600 silk-looms in Vienna alone, and in Styria 300,000 cwt. of bar iron is wrought. Of remarkable railways, I will mention only one which runs over the Simering mountain, which is 3,200 feet high; this railroad, in a space of $32\frac{1}{4}$ English miles, is carried over eleven viaducts, and through thirteen tunnels, one of which is 8,400 feet long. In the latter part of 1850, Austria had 1,250 English miles of railroad running through her dominions. If we consider that all this working power is in the hands of Germans, and that Hungary, in spite of the richness of its soil, is hardly even nominally represented in the field of industrial activity, we shall see in these statistics only a further confirmation of what I for truth's sake have asserted in my answers to M. Szemere's work.

I do not despair of Hungary's future, as soon as it can be brought to acknowledge its true position and mission. Let every Hungarian begin the regeneration of his country with himself; let him employ his aristocratic and national enthusiasm in improving the situation of the masses of the people, by commerce, trade, agriculture,—even at the expense of personal sacrifices; let him educate himself as well as the poorer orders of the people; and with the growth of moral and intellectual freedom, political freedom will undoubtedly ensue. But as long as this is not the case,—as long as real improvement is sacrificed to imaginary dreams of Magyar supremacy, in whose hands, according to certain visionary schemers, lies the future fate of Austria and Turkey,—we shall only witness the growth of that civilization which I have described in the following pages.

Should I be reviled by all parties in Hungary, it will only be in consequence of having told the truth; but the present moment is too important to allow anyone to remain silent, when by a few truthful remarks, he may, perhaps, promote the real development of his country.

LONDON, May 26th, 1860.

CIVILIZATION IN HUNGARY.

ANSWER I.

Sir,

You have honoured Mr. Cobden, M.P. for Rochdale, with seven letters, for which, I have no doubt, he was most delighted to find room in some odd out-of-the-way corner, devoted to *unimportant matters*; for what can the Honourable Member for Rochdale have to do with Hungary? Has he ever had either a commercial or social connection with Hungary? Is Hungary of more consequence to him than Otaheitee or any other insignificant little island?

Mankind, more especially that part of it occupying the British Isles, improves from day to day, holding only to that which is practicable and possible, above all to that which is true. Truth must be the foundation of every political discussion, or else the discussion is wanting in vitality.

In addressing your complaints to an English Member of Parliament, who cannot be capable of judging of the merits of your case, you do not think it necessary to adhere too closely to the truth, which, in your career as minister of a *free* Government, you have doubtless found as troublesome as any servant of a despot.

Through the Press, your letters have become public property, and I look upon it as a sacred duty to give a candid answer to each of your seven letters. I love the land about which you write, no less than yourself. Like you, I have smiled, prayed, struggled, and suffered there; but, thank Heaven, I have never occupied the position of a minister, and therefore I have not helped to compass its ruin; neither am I a noble, but only a man of the people, simply an impartial studious observer, who, after long and earnest thought, has been obliged to come to this conclusion, viz., that nations led astray by party-spirit, work their own unhappiness by seeking for the cause of their physical and social dependence where it is not to be found.

It is my intention to lay the same subject, viewed from a different side, before the English people, and I will leave them to decide which of us has paid the greatest homage to the genius of truth, and which view is likely to be most profitable, both to the people at home and the people abroad.

The statistics given in the Introduction to your seven letters prove two things: firstly, that the Magyars are in the minority, when the rest of the population of Hungary, whom you are pleased to term "Races," are taken together; secondly, that the Germans of Hungary are superior in intelligence to the rest of the population.* Why you should give the high-sounding title of nation only to the Magyars, when, by your own showing, they are inferior in number to the other inhabitants of Hungary, is to me unaccountable; and your admission

* I must here correct a mistake you have made in your statements concerning books and public newspapers. You wish to prove to the world by your numbers, that the literary taste of Hungary is only on the side of the Magyars, and to support this, you say that there are many more books and newspapers in the Magyar language than in the German; but you forget, or rather you do not choose to remember, how many books are imported from Austria and Germany. If you had wished to be just and correct, you would have named the journals and works from Vienna, Berlin, Leipzig, Hamburg, and Augsburg that are circulated in Hungary. I should advise you to compare the importation of German with the exportation of Hungarian works.

of the fact, that the Germans send 80 per cent. of their children to school, whilst all the other nations remain far below this standard, shows in what direction civilization is making most progress.

Cultivation and instruction are the first rounds in the ladder, which every nation must ascend before it can be possessed of internal and unfailing sources of wealth,—before it can be made ready for freedom. These simple facts will prove to a man of Mr. Cobden's powers that it is a fatal mistake to give the supremacy to the Magyars, who care less for education, manufactures, commerce, and labour in general than the rest of the population.

It is the greatest misfortune for the Magyars that, through a long range of eventful centuries, they have never possessed a single statesman fit to fill a higher position than that of a local politician, always excepting the great and immortal Count Széchényi, whose brilliant capabilities were obscured by insanity, till he put an end to his life by suicide. Széchényi was indeed a bright exception; he was the first to introduce English ideas of government into Hungary. But when did he do this? After nearly eight hundred years of indolent neglect on the part of the Magyars; for all the grandeur of their past is confined to the glorious deeds of the Middle Ages, which, like the wonderful victories of a Tamerlane or an Attila, now signify *nothing.*

The towns were built by the industry of strangers, the commerce was in the hands of the Germans, the Servians, the Slaves, and the Jews, for the Magyar noble considered trade of any description as a disgrace. You might constantly hear such speeches as the following issue from their lips with quiet pride: "My ancestors never worked, and shall I work? No! I will rather die than so disgrace myself."

The Magyar schools were bad, only calculated to bring out mediocre talent. Those who were by nature highly endowed, turned to Germany in olden times, just as much as they do now. The reforms, that during the last thirty years have surprised us, have found us still struggling with the abuses of the Middle Ages. The remnants of Magyarism, which are to be found in dusty old pandects, and in the Tripartitum, the Hungarian law-book, show traces of the worst kind of despotism, the most humiliating and inhuman oppression of all human rights, and now you come forward, and by your letters increase these wrongs. You do not complain of the past; but you excuse that which deserves no excuse. You not only excuse it, but you embellish it. You conceal every defect, every iniquity. You strike from the tablets of your memory all that is unfavourable to the Magyars; and by your pleading for the future of Hungary, you misrepresent the history of the past and present. It is no longer a secret to the thinkers of every country, that history proves that the fate of nations is ruled by certain and unalterable laws. Is it, then, right for you to try and make people believe that Hungary is to be an exception to these unalterable laws? Will this servile flattery show the Magyars the error of their ways? Will it lessen their defects? Will it help them to repent of the sins committed during the last eight centuries, and prevent their repetition? No; but I will endeavour to rescue the honour of the Hungarian patriots, by pointing out their failings; and though a native of the same country as yourself, I will prove to them that I am capable of seeing their faults, and dare to acknowledge them, and I will bring well-known historical facts to the support of my argument.

In olden times it was considered necessary to convince nations that all that fed their presumption and flattered their childish vanity was true.

But this is not the case. There is a higher standard than flattery by which the truth must be tested, viz., intellect, which tries alike the past and present, emperors and kings, individuals and people.

In order that I may make your letters and my answers understood by the English public, I must be allowed to describe the different positions from which we view the past, present, and future of Hungary.

You write as a late minister, and, therefore, you must have looked upon passing events with the circumscribed vision of a government official. You have most likely gleaned what knowledge you possess from official despatches. Your reasoning is that of a one-sided party-man, who looks back with regret to the time when an unjust constitution, and the privileges of his birth, called him to play a part in the politics of the day. You write as the blind worshipper of the greatest living despot, under whose rule all freedom of speech and liberty of the press is forbidden; of a man who strives by juggling tricks to loosen the legitimate bonds of Europe; who is ignorant of the binding nature of an oath; who has looked north, south, east, and west for allies, but finding none to answer his purpose, as a last resource he appeals to the passions of the populace, before whom he waves the flimsy rag of "Independent National Rights," and endeavours to hide the tyrannical oppression at home, by continually agitating foreign countries in a manner calculated to disturb the normal development of Europe. Your letters are full of that phraseology which belongs to the French people, who are content with words, not deeds; who are ever easily satisfied with a few sublime sentences about liberty.

I will endeavour to base my answers upon history, and a true description of the social condition of Hungary; and I will add, that I am an open enemy of class or race interests, which produce relations like that of the Spartan to the Helot, the Magyar to the other races (to use your own expression), the planter to the negro.

I write my answer in a land where *truth*, even amid the struggles of opposing political parties, always finds a hearing; for it is the land of freedom, where in the constant contemplation of the surrounding sea, "the idea of the indefinite, the unlimited and infinite, stimulate and embolden men to stretch beyond the limited;" where the mean appears more mean; where man, conscious of his inborn power, surveys *the world*, and does not look at it with the narrowness of a local politician; where nations are valued according to their knowledge, their thinking men, their discoveries, their manufactures, the extension of their trade; where, with all due respect for the aristocracy, INTELLECT is acknowledged to be the moving spring of the State; where a future is gradually opening for the masses, when these masses shall have become virtuous, honest, persevering, and capable of ever keeping the one object in view,— that they are to form a part of a harmonious whole.

You speak of the Hungarian constitution as "so admirably adapted to the development of individual talent, as a model of local self-government, a nursery of patriots, a palladium of liberties, an arena of daily struggles, a practical school for magistrates and statesmen;" but you forget to give Mr. Cobden an idea of either the nature or extent of the constitution. You forget that this constitution was only for 500,000 people; that these 500,000 people were all nobles; that the electors as well as the elected were nobles; that these nobles did not bear any of the burdens of the State; paid no duties, no imposts, no taxes; that they were never required to do military duty, except when the whole country was called upon to take up arms, in times of pressing danger; that 14,000,000 people paid duties, imposts, taxes, and served as soldiers for these 500,000 nobles; and yet this admirably developed constitution gave them no privileges, afforded them no protection against being flogged or shot, if it so pleased the nobles.

With what horror must a man like Mr. Cobden look upon this *liberal constitution!*—a man who is of obscure birth, and only risen to be a member of the Parliament of the first and greatest nation of the world by reason of his talents. How will he view the past, present, and future of Hungary, when he reads that, the Decretum I. art. lxxix., and the Decretum III. art. x. Charles III., were only repealed towards the middle of the last century?—those laws which forbade merchants and handicraftsmen to over- or under-sell their wares;—and, consequently, that commerce and progress were hindered, instead of assisted, by the constitution. This alone will show a statesman of our own time, more especially a free-trader like the Honourable Member for Rochdale, where the stumbling-block of improvement and civilization did lie. But what will Mr. Cobden, what will Englishmen say, when we tell them that the misfortunes of Hungary originated in the constitution forbidding the tax-paying part of the population to possess any immovable property; and that these hard-working bearers of the State burdens were legally branded as "*misera plebs contribuens.*" * What would Englishmen think if their lord mayors and aldermen were pointed at as "*misera plebs contribuens?*" — ("the wretched contributing mob!")

Do you not feel and know that an injustice of this description, committed by a handful of Asiatic warriors, who, coming from the Caucasus, brought to the people on the Danube neither milder customs, more elevated virtues, nor a nobler government,—do you not feel and know that an injustice of this description must sooner or later bring its own punishment? Countries that have been originally conquered by the sword can no longer be ruled by the sword, as they might have been, and were, 1000 years back. Do you not think that there must be something radically wrong in a State which shows no sign of improvement after

* Verböczi Tripartitum, pars i., tit. 9; Charles III. Decretum II. art. v. vi., and Maria Theresia I. art. viii.

an existence of eight centuries? Was it mere chance that the roads were impassable, the trade insignificant, the Government approaching nearer to that of the Pasha's in cruelty and oppression than any other in Europe?

You surely cannot but think that a law which commands boiling oil to be poured down the throat of the Sudras or Pariah, should he dare to read in the holy books, must have its influence on the social and intellectual development of a State! It is the same with nations as with individuals. If an individual bases his acts on wrong principles, his whole existence is as the links of an unconnected chain. If the fundamental laws of a land are based upon false principles, it is impossible for that land to develope itself; it will stand still, even though on all sides resounds the cry of "Excelsior!" Such a country can no longer excite even common interest in the modern world, for it belongs to a time when knights-errant, and all the gorgeous nonsensical parade of a tournament, delighted mankind; but that has long lost all charm for us, because it was aimless, and had no *intellectual* life.

When the aristocracy of a land condemns the working, producing classes to slavery, when it checks all industry and trade, the two principal sources of a country's prosperity, by holding them up to the scorn of those who are forced upon the nation as its rulers, statesmen would be wrong to seek for the cause of the ruin of their country in external relations: they must look for the cause of its being incapable of keeping pace with other nations in its own institutions, and if they are not blinded by partiality, they will be sure to find it.

The division of property, the right regulation of wages, the relative positions of the working classes to their employers, the peasant to his lord, are of the greatest importance in the development of a State. It is a well-known fact that in those countries where the food is cheap, and the climate temperate, the working classes are the poorest, and the gap between them and the landholders is almost insurmountable. In such countries the peasant is nothing more than a beast of burden; the labourer and servant are held under by means of the whip or the knout;—kicks and blows move the machinery of the State.

Let us glance at the Egypt, India, and Peru of olden times. In none of these lands was the despotism that of one man; no! it was class despotism, which is more oppressive, more bloody, and more intolerable than that of a single tyrant. When we admire those extraordinary antiquities, the pyramids of the Egyptians, the catacombs, and the mausoleums, we show our ignorance of State philosophy. Those marvels are the melancholy monuments of a social condition that allowed a few to oppress the masses of the people and convert them into beasts of burden.

Egypt, India, and Peru made a fearful mistake in the division of the material as well as political power between the privileged and the unprivileged classes; consequently these once prosperous, aye, even civilized, States, have disappeared from the face of the political world. Egypt is a vast churchyard, in which palaces are the tombstones. India is fortunately in the hands of a wise conqueror. Peru exists only in name. There is a great resemblance in the legal and political organization of these three countries and that of Hungary; therefore I cannot understand why you or any one else should be astonished at the results which show themselves as effects of certain causes.

Without even taking into account either the circumstances of the times or the geographical position of Egypt, India, and Peru, it must be acknowledged that civilization had reached a very high standard in those countries. The Egyptians were one of the most learned of all nations before the Christian era; and though later they were surpassed in philosophy by the Greeks, yet the Greeks themselves used *their* discoveries of the laws of astronomy as the foundation of all their own. The Indians possess a literature hardly inferior to our own in beauty and the depth and subtilty of its philosophy. But notwithstanding this, no vitality was in these nations, because the germ of progress was wanting, because the higher classes were too isolated, and the lower classes sunk in the mire of the profoundest slavery and ignorance.

Although you say that "There is only one country in Europe where the Slave and the Wallac *races* enjoy constitutional liberty, and could, if they wished, freely cultivate their own languages and retain their national customs," yet I maintain that neither the Wallac nor the German, the Greek nor the Croat, the Armenian nor the Hungarian, enjoyed anything approaching to constitutional freedom; it is only the Magyar nobles that were thus distinguished. I need merely mention an historical fact in support of this assertion. In 1741, the natives of Dalmatia, Croatia, and

Slavonia, were declared noble Magyars, and as far as regarded dignities, offices, and benefices, were placed upon an equal footing with the native *nobles* of Hungary ;* and to maintain the dignity of the *country nobility*, as well as that of the magnates, they were allowed—but only with the permission of the king—to entail any newly-acquired estates.† Your assertion would have been a just one, if you had not forgotten to mention, that this admirable constitution was created only for the Magyar nobles, and that to make those foreign tribes equally worthy of this freedom by birth, they actually condescended to turn those foreigners into Magyar nobles !

What a different colouring this gives to your high-sounding sentence about the liberty enjoyed by all who lived under Hungarian rule. By this magnanimous act of the Magyars, it would appear that, like the Jews, they wished to create a national individuality superior to that of all other nations; not in vain did they, as the Israelites, boast of a peculiar Jehovah, a " Magyarok Istene," a Magyar God.

It is certainly true that, at the end of June,

---

* Maria Theresia, Decret. I. art. xli. and lii.
† Car. III. Decret. II. art. L

1849, *i. e.*, at the end of the struggle for freedom, *equal rights* were proclaimed by the Hungarian Diet at Szegedin for all the different nationalities. Do you think, by your denial of all preceding historical facts, that the poor Wallacs and Slaves, and Servians and Croats, had already enjoyed those rights for centuries, which were only granted to them at the end of our triumphs by a sublime or, rather, timid generosity.

Will you never be able to comprehend how matters stand? Will you and the Magyar party always remain blind to the evidence which history offers? There must have been a cause for the hatred that in 1849 impregnated Hungary's fruitful fields with blood. You point at the Austrian government as that cause, but I deny this most completely. A non-resident government cannot have very much power over a country, which, according to your own showing, was blessed with a constitution which, in wisdom and justice, far surpassed that of Switzerland or the United States. Have Englishmen ever thought of holding Queen Victoria and her ministers responsible for the late rebellion in India? And yet the government of the Queen of England was more closely connected with the Indian administration in 1857 than the

Austrian Government was with the administration of Hungary in 1848.

Hungary is alone the cause of its own misfortunes. It was governed by the same excellent constitution 500 years before it fell under the dominion of the Austrian. Was it then in a better condition? Was Austria the cause of the disaster at Mohacs; or was it chance that brought about that dreadful catastrophe? It is impossible to acknowledge the power of chance in the historical development of a people. We know that all events are subject to universal laws. The disaster at Mohacs was the concluding act of the Magyar independence-drama. Lewis II. was unable to find either money or soldiers for the defence of his kingdom, even when Sultan Soliman was knocking at the very gates of Peterwárdein, the Gibraltar of Hungary. The nobles were, as usual, at variance with one another, the prelates and magnates would do nothing, and the people, groaning under the heaviest oppression, in consequence of the rebellion of the peasants under Dozsa, listened with the coldest indifference to the demand for soldiers and money to rescue their tyrants from the ferocious Turks. Nothing could increase their own misery, and who could expect those who had no rights to lose, to defend the rights of their oppressors?

The Government officials plundered whenever they were able; the commandant of Zengh, Gregory Orlowich, sold the corn which Pope Adrian VI. sent for the support of the garrison of this frontier fortress of Croatia. The States promised taxes and soldiers, and the monasteries promised money. But promises alone could not save the unhappy country. The king was advised to solicit foreign princes to assist him with their forces, for they had already found room in their hearts for the suicidal principle of allowing strangers to fight for their hearths and homes. Even the powerful John Zapolya did not bestir himself in this overwhelming danger, which threatened the utter annihilation of a country over which he hoped one day to reign. Henry VIII. of England sent a large sum of money, which Pope Clement VII. increased to 50,000 ducats; but, in spite of all this, the king was obliged to compel his nobles to appear in the field, by threatening to punish as traitors all who did not answer his summons.

This admirable constitution of the Magyars deprived the unhappy Lewis II. of all foreign sympathy, and of the support of his subjects.

He saw himself surrounded by hostile governments, yet he was without an official who would obey his orders; his council wanted both judgment and unanimity; he was without ships on the Danube, and had not a single man fit to command a hundred soldiers, much less a whole army; and yet Soliman and his 300,000 warriors were before the gates. Bloody swords were carried through town and village, but in vain. Citizen and peasant looked at them with scornful indifference, and watched with malicious joy the near approach of danger; for what had these "*misera plebs contribuens*" to lose?—Nothing!

The Hungarian government officials, worthy pillars of this admirable constitution, defrauded the royal treasury to such an infamous extent, that the Nuncio del Burgio was obliged to supply 92 ducats for the journey of the Provost Bebek, who was sent to persuade the Palatine and the nobles to unite in suppressing the danger.* At last the king with a heavy heart confronted the enemy with very inferior forces: he sustained a most disastrous defeat, and, having fallen from his horse, was drowned in the brook of Csellye!

* Anton Pullen del Burgio to Sadolet at Buda. See "Pray. Epist. Procer." Part. I. p. 243.

Twenty thousand Hungarians, amongst whom was the flower of the nobility, covered the field of battle. On that day the great Spirit of the Universe chastised the lordly caste that had sought nothing but its own advancement. The Hungarian nobles saw themselves forsaken by the people, scorned by the citizens, cheated by their friends, and defrauded by their officials; for they had ruled over the land, not by right of intellectual superiority, but of arbitrary privileges, which history tells us that they had won for themselves, not by any intellectual superiority, but by the sword! Now modern philosophers, historians, and statesmen, who watch the progress of mankind earnestly, look for the results of the spread of knowledge among a people, and at the state of civilization in which an historical period may surprise them.

Let us compare Hungary at this period with England under Charles II., a dissipated king without either intellect or talent. England was a continual prey to conspiracies at home; and abroad she was treated with scorn and contempt. "To all this were added two natural calamities of the most grievous description, — a great plague, which thinned society in all its ranks, and scattered confusion through the kingdom; and a great fire, which, besides increasing the mortality from the pestilence, destroyed in a moment those accumulations of industry by which industry itself is nourished. If we put all these things together, how can we reconcile inconsistencies apparently so gross? How could so wonderful a progress be made in the face of these unparalleled disasters? How could men under such circumstances effect such improvements?"*

And how is it that Hungary did not progress in civilization? How is it that the only period in which the arts and sciences flourished in Hungary, and then only with the help of *foreign* authors and learned men, was when Matthias Corvinus *tyrannically oppressed the nobles?* How is it that Hungary, in spite of its constitutional government, remained stationary in its social and intellectual development? I will answer you in the words of the greatest living historian in England, a man whose universal intellect penetrates through mankind, countries, and centuries, and at once gives the key to every historical phenomenon. "The history of every civilized country is the history of its intellectual development, which kings, statesmen, and legislators are more likely to retard than

* Buckle's "History of Civilization in England," p. 354.

to hasten; because, however great their power may be, they are at the best the accidental and insufficient representatives of their times; ... while beyond them, and on every side of them, are forming *opinions* and *principles* which they can scarcely perceive, but by which alone the whole course of human affairs is ultimately governed."* What are these opinions and principles? Where, and through whom, are they to be brought out? This I will treat of in my second Answer.

* Buckle's "History of Civilization in England," vol. i. p. 351.

ANSWER II.

People generally look upon a government as representing opposite interests to the public; they never understand clearly that the power of the government is only their own power, that the opinions of the government are the opinions of the majority of the people. The "statesphilosophers" are obliged to look at the opinions and principles of society in order to discover those of a government. "The revealed history of the inner life of a nation," says a French sage, "is the history either of the virtues or the defects of their rulers; kings martyr the people." That is possible when the rulers of a people are despots. But you allow that, till 1848, Hungary possessed the best and most liberal constitutional government—the one, in fact, that approached nearest to that of England. The above sentence cannot possibly have any reference to constitutional governments; for the State in which it is possible for a ruler to be a tyrant is not in possession of a constitutional government. In constitutional countries the people are martyrs to their own mismanagement. However kings may help to demoralize a people, they can only do it where the people are themselves sunk in the lowest depths of depravity.

For centuries Englishmen suffered from the caprice of ambitious monarchs; but intellectual, thinking men shook the masses out of their lethargy: a trade was created; by trade riches were amassed—and rich and independent citizens can never be oppressed.

France lay like a slave at the feet of a centralized despotism, till the Encyclopædists awoke her. But the intellectual lords of the slave forgot to lay faith and morality as the corner-stone of their State, and in spite of the rivers of blood that were shed, the building that arose on the banks of the Seine crumbled and fell.

The dreamy Germans were long an object of intellectual oppression; but, since the Reformation, their intellectual and literary development has reached an elevation of which an Englishman speaks with generous impartiality, in the following terms:—" As to the Germans, it is undoubtedly true that, since the middle of the eighteenth century, they have produced a greater number of profound thinkers than any other country,—I might, perhaps, say, than all other countries put together."* Germany possesses in every direction the material for development: it is the mission of Germany to be the prop of European freedom.

But what material do the Magyars, as a State, furnish towards the future development of civilization?

Whoever looks upon him who is not blind to the defects of his country as an enemy of the same, is himself the greatest enemy of what he professes to love. Nations never progress if their errors are concealed; but if they once begin to listen to the voice of truth, however harsh, there is hope that time will bring them into the only onward course.

"Nosce te ipsum,"—first learn to know your own character, your neighbours, the means and sources of your calling, your wants, and how and through whom these may be satisfied, and then begin to build your house and furnish it; thus, in time, you will lose your childish dreams, and spare your physical and mental powers for the reality of life. To strive for freedom is not suffi-

* Buckle's "History of Civilization in England," vol. i., p. 217.

cient in itself. The demonstrations of a few students have never succeeded in making a people free. Tailors' bills for embroidered coats cannot save a country. Not the shorn locks, but the independent *principles* which the men professed who were honoured by the name of "Roundheads," made England free. Hungary must have a future; but this future will never be reached either by means of Magyarism or Mr. Cobden,—least of all with the assistance of H. I. M. Napoleon III.

Hungary must break off all connexion with the past. Every Magyar—every individual born in Hungary—must reform. The cause of the common evil is only to be found in each individuality.

In your Second Letter you assert, with extraordinary certainty, that Hungary was a free and independent kingdom, since the year 893. In my first answer I have merely recorded historical facts, in order to show you what condition Hungary was in, when it ceased to exist as an independent kingdom. Torn by contending factions, and nearly conquered by the Turks, it was only too glad to throw itself into the arms of the Austrians.

It is now my intention to give you a sketch of

Hungary's social condition, from my own observations and experience, which may, perhaps, bring back to your memory under what circumstances the Hungarian movement of 1848 surprised us; for your letters are truly great in all that they disguise, or altogether conceal.

Ever since the seven Hero-Chiefs, at the head of their Magyar forces, took possession of Pannonia, treason, hate, private and party interests, have been the curse of this *free* country. In the battle-field the Magyars were ever irreproachable, for they are heroes by birth. Generous enthusiasm, though, unfortunately an enthusiasm of a very evanescent nature, heats every drop of a Magyar's blood; but in social and political life they have always wanted calmness, firmness, and an insight into the true position of affairs. None of the race but looked upon industry of any description with undisguised contempt: the arts and sciences have only been thought of during the last thirty years. Here, again, history stamps upon my assertion the impress of truth. Though the tricolor of the Magyars was once planted on the battlements of Vienna by Matthias Corvinus, yet we see that same tricolor trampled in the dust at Mohacs. To-day, Rakotzy presses hard on the Imperialists, but dissension in his own camp compels him to withdraw from the scene of action; and but a short space of time elapses before we see him forsaken and alone, writing his Memoirs upon Turkish ground. I shall have occasion to speak of these Memoirs in my fourth Letter.

The fate of Hungary, under the rule of the Magyars, was continually fluctuating: there was nothing firm or intellectual to fall back upon; there was no gradual improvement in its commerce; nothing but daring and bloody ventures, and still more bloody losses,—to-day, a lavish, pomp-loving State; to-morrow, a desert, which Turks and Tartars water with Christian blood;—yesterday, in the bonds of feudalism; to-morrow, dreaming of a republic based upon St. Simonian principles;—everywhere frightful precipices and roaring torrents, but nowhere is a bridge to be seen by which these precipices and torrents might be safely passed.

And what was the cause of this evil?

My answer will probably disgust you—you will look upon it as a paradox; but I feel convinced that Mr. Cobden, from what I have already said, will consider it a just one.

The cause of the miseries of Hungary, during

its existence as an independent kingdom, as well as since its submission to the house of Habsburg, was *its abnormal constitution*. How ridiculous does the Duke of Baden appear, of whom A. Von Humboldt relates the following anecdote in one of his letters:—"When his Grace counted his guests before sitting down to dinner, he discovered that there were thirteen; but he comforted himself quickly with this reflection, 'There are, in fact, only eleven, for the two commoners count as nought!'" And this was the opinion legally asserted by the Magyars in their constitutional code. How could thus have been developed any public opinion in order to support and to lead the State, or to assist the government and to promote progress, and to render possible the free development of Hungary, notwithstanding the polyglot mass of nobles and commoners—of lords and slaves? The noble was first in life, in State, in society—yes, even in the Church. Everyone who wore a respectable coat, provided he was not a burgher or a peasant, was a Herr *von*. Till 1848, neither the citizen nor the peasant was, in fact, represented in this excellent constitution. What does Abbé Siéyes say?—" 'What is the citizen?' 'Nothing.' 'But what shall he be?' 'Everything!'" Do you believe that Louis Napoleon, who makes the *soldier* the "everything" of France, is the man to understand the future of Europe? This question I intend to answer in my sixth Letter.

What has the Magyar constitution done for the citizen and the peasant?

It robbed the "*misera plebs contribuens*" of every political right, and thus sowed dissension in the State, which was an insurmountable obstacle to its development, and made the land, for nearly a thousand years, the scene of bloody feuds; its aristocracy caring as little for the Austrian Government as it did for the rights of the commoner, only assisting the former in its oppression of the masses; so that Austria, in order to win a party for itself, was actually obliged to play the part of a modern liberal, and side with the people.

Let us look at all ranks in society, from the magnate down to the peasant, what was their condition before 1848? There was no cement by which the heterogeneous masses could be bound together for the welfare of the whole.

We will begin with the magnates. They included all the princes, counts, bishops, prelates, and barons of the Empire. These pomp-loving magnates were, with very few exceptions, humbly devoted to the Austrian Court. As long as the Court loaded them with honours, and did not interfere with their own particular privileges, everything went on smoothly. The magnates (again I must add with some exceptions) distinguished themselves only by their blind self-conceit, seeking their own grandeur in proud contempt of the commoner, and caring only for their own charters. Jealous even of the Government which permitted them to live at the expense of the peasant and the citizen, they only protected the latter when the taxes were so heavy, and the levy of soldiers so constant, that it threatened to injure their own purse, either directly or indirectly. The education of these scions of aristocracy made them disregard human rights in general, and those of the commoner in particular. They learnt Latin, French, German, and, since 1830, a very little of the Magyar language. They contented themselves with studying at their own wretched schools, in a most superficial manner, and then they were supposed fit for the most important posts of the State; and even these were sometimes part of their inheritance, consequently, they could not always fall to the lot of the most capable.

These magnates opposed every step towards improvement on the part of the people, and hindered, by their intrigues and indolence, any inclination for progress on the part of the higher classes. The history of the kings and ministers of this unhappy country shows that the magnates always waged a deadly war against the interests of the people, or, as in more modern times, they only made use of these interests for their own selfish purposes. Occasionally, indeed, we see a meteor shoot across the leaden clouds which hovered over this unhappy land,—for instance, a Zriny and Hunyadi;—but Hungary has never given birth to a Kepler, Guttenberg, Hans Sachs, Luther, Kant, Schiller, Goethe, Humboldt, or whatever the numberless representatives of German science, German progress, German industry, or German discoveries, may be called. Hungary, as long as it was an independent kingdom, was the theatre of ambitious stratagems on the part of those who lived upon the sweat of the people's brows. The enlargement of their family estates, and the increase of their own glory was the moving-spring of many a great and political agitation,—the cause of many a seeming martyrdom for the rights of the people, or of a treacherous and tyrannical oppression of the same. However brave and noble the Magyar might be upon the battle-field, he was ambitious and short-sighted at the council-table, and the scourge of those beneath his class: thus he robbed the State of those elements without which no kingdom can exist, or develope itself regularly. Arts, sciences, and commercial enterprizes were held in contempt, because these things were considered unworthy of the attention of a magnate. Educated in foreign tongues, the magnate early learnt to admire all that was foreign; but, in their intercourse with foreigners, they imitated only that which was superficial. I think it must be clear, even to you, that, under such circumstances, it was impossible for the people in the kingdom, who dared not have a public opinion, to assist in the development of the State. When the majorats (entailed estates) were partly abolished, many magnates became poor; but their taste for an idle life of splendour did not disappear at the same time with their riches. The desire to keep up the magnificence of their establishments induced them to accept places at court, and government situations of all kinds; for, as commerce was beneath them, this was their only resource. The salaries of the county-officials were so small* that, to enable them to maintain their dignity, they all were obliged to demand legal, more especially, however, illegal "fees." Bribery and corruption stalked unblushingly in the noonday glare, opening every gate and door, and demoralizing the nation. If a judge had accepted little or nothing from the opposing parties, he would have been looked upon as a natural curiosity. Diogenes would have sought in vain for such an individual. The practical good sense of the English aristocracy, which never obstinately opposed the commoners when it might be dangerous to the State, and the self-devotion of the German, who does not hesitate to sacrifice his life to the commands of honour, were utterly wanting in the Magyar: he combined the mocking scepticism of the Frenchman with the strutting grandeur of the Spanish hidalgo, and the indolence of the Pasha. Coarse, unpoetical materialism, or dark superstition, were the distinguishing features of the higher classes: they looked upon religion, intellect, and improvement, as ornaments which might be easily dispensed with. The love of Oriental luxury,

* A *Vice-Gespann* (Lord Lieutenant) received about £60 per annum, and he was obliged to spend at least four times as much in table-money.

without the common sense of the western world, and the frivolities of chivalry, conceit, imitation of all that was French, and horror of any work that required exertion, were the characteristics of those among the Magyars who could boast of the most ancient names and titles.

And these were the men who held the most important offices in the state, and were in possession of all the political power and the landed property. It was the house of magnates which was the stumbling-block to all progress. Every wish, every little sigh for improvement, retreated, crest-fallen, from before the wall with which the peculiar privileges of caste surrounded the magnates. They possessed more than five-eighths of the land; and what was the state of agriculture, and what were the means of communication, when the Revolution of 1848 took place? They would have had command of the most money if a ridiculous prodigality had not obliged them, frequently, to sell the fleeces off their sheep, and their crops of corn, three, even six years beforehand. Where are the museums, libraries, schools, and public buildings, which ought to belong to a free and independent nation? Foreigners built, with the help of foreign money, the suspension-bridge which unites Buda and Pesth; the rail-roads are in the hands of foreigners; the steam navigation of the Danube and Black Sea belongs entirely to foreigners. The great lords ordered everything from Paris,— that is to say, if they were in possession of ready money; if not, they were content to get them on credit at Vienna: they supported the manufactures of their own country with contemptuous sneers only.

This aristocracy was worthily supported by the proud, unbending Roman Catholic clergy. In no country in the world was the Romish clergy, comparatively, so rich as in Hungary; but,—except during the Middle Ages, when they succeeded in giving new life to the Greek and Romish classics,—the clergy never did, or would assist in the intellectual development of the people. This was not the fault of the clergy, but of the construction of the Romish hierarchy. The most liberal monarch that ever ascended a throne, Joseph II., wished to reform the Romish Church of Hungary; but the static party opposed the attempts of the Emperor. The Primate of the kingdom, Cardinal Batthyanyi,* would not acknowledge that anything wrong could exist in the

* See Katona's "History of Hungary," Vol. XI., p. 92.

Church. Although the Emperor gave all those clergymen who could not conscientiously obey him permission to resign their official appointments, and retire from the kingdom, yet these conscientious gentlemen preferred parting with their scruples to giving up their comfortable posts, and were content with organizing secret opposition to the emperor. The prelate of Hungary made use of the temporal, as well as the spiritual power. He was more often in the cabinet than in the pulpit. Occasionally, he even used the sword, when the crozier was powerless in effecting his will. That which the temporal magnate neglected to sacrifice to his private interests, the spiritual lord seized as his own share of the spoil, and made the State and civilization subservient to the principle of "the end sanctifies the means." These magnates formed the static element of Hungary, and did not trouble themselves to find out the dynamic powers of the intellect, in order to promote the progressive education of the people. Traditions were carefully preserved; knowledge of every kind that might tend to diminish the blind faith of the people was excluded from their circle. But, in spite of all this, they were *tolerant*, for the management of their large estates did not allow them time for theological controversy. If an Hungarian king would but have secured them their estates by becoming Protestant, he would have succeeded in converting these tolerant prelates even into followers of Mahomet, if such had been his pleasure. You accuse Austria of having wished to make Hungary poor and Catholic; but the high caste of the Magyars did this, for though magnates, prelates, and nobles were the only possessors of the fruitful land, yet they did nothing towards the improvement of agriculture, commercial enterprise, or home manufactures. Why, then, did this liberal constitution give all its privileges to men who assisted neither the intellectual nor material developement of the land?

The most compact power in the State was composed of the lower class of nobility, *i.e.* the simple Herrn Von, who were a kind of French gentilhomme. The nation was represented by two Houses of Parliament: the magnates sat in the Upper, the Herrn Von in the Lower House; and, as I have before stated, the representatives of the Lower House were only elected by nobles. An inclination for general improvement, but more often hatred of the magnates or a mere love of opposition, induced the nobles to protect the commoners. It is certainly worthy of notice that the unprivileged part of the nation was generally the bone of contention in both houses.

The nobles found themselves in rather a singular position, in consequence of the injustice of their own constitution. According to their rights they were above the people, but by their opposition to the magnates they placed themselves on an equality with them: the latter, however, never made sincerely common cause with them; they suspected the intention of the nobles, and feared to be made use of as a means to some selfish end. To this want of confidence must be added the obstacle which the difference of nationalities placed in the way of united efforts. The nobility were for the most part *Magyars*, and by their hasty, ill-directed efforts for a separate nationality, which they hoped to advance by *legal* instead of *social* means, they aroused the bitterest animosity in the various nationalities of which the State was composed, and induced them to elevate the standard of revolt. The Magyar nobility, ever since they settled in Europe, had always reserved the *pursuit* of politics for their own exclusive right. They imagined that because the constitution permitted it that it was but the just reward of their services to the State, and that these services, which they esteemed very highly, made them peculiarly adapted for the political management, not only of the Magyars, but of the other nations who submitted to their rule. They complained bitterly of the indifference of the German, Wallac, etc. to all political matters, forgetting that they were legally deprived of every political right. Instead of removing the evil they contented themselves with thinking it incurable. In spite of all this the Lower House formed the only real opposition to the old system, and the " Bulla Aurea" constitution. It was in consequence of the abnormal condition of the State that the nobility, with heroic self-devotion, attacked their own peculiar privileges; they cast them off so that they might give to those who had none. The nobility of the nineteenth century began to be ashamed of their unjust rights, which they felt they could not retain without sinning against every law, human and divine; but in their endeavours to transfer them to their fellow countrymen they made a fatal mistake, which for ever endangered the supremacy of the Magyars. They sought to attain their just wishes by "*denationalizing*" every other people under the dominion of Hungary. They proposed that every man, who by his position was entitled to his political emancipation, should only receive the same on condition that he *abjured his language.* The good that the nobility wished to do in one way, they neutralized in another. The political future that they wished to build, was without foundation; it fell because the principle contradicted the practical possibility!

But in our abnormal constitution was yet another genus of nobility, which combined the ancient feudal customs with those of the modern democrats; this was the Sandal-nobility. This Sandal or rather peasant nobility were the same to the political improvement of Hungary as the Condottieris in the Middle Ages were to the public safety; they occupied the same position which enabled the Janissaries of the Turks to render Reform impossible. They possessed the same privileges as the richer nobility, but their poverty held them enchained; as they were entirely without serfs, they were obliged to plough their own fields, and drive their own cattle. In spite of this they were favoured above common mortals; they were little kings in their own fields, and their mud huts were their palaces.

When you quoted Lord Chatham upon Hungary you forgot to refer to the Tripartitum, where you would have found the following passage, mentioning the rights and liberties of the *people* :

"Nomine autem populi hoc in loco intellige solummodo dominos, prelatos, barones, et alios magnates, atque quostibet nobiles."

This nobility had just as much right to vote either for Members of Parliament, or Government Officials, as the magnates or Herrn Von. These Bocskoros* were distinguished by their roughness and arrogance; they scorned the peasant whom the laws of this noble constitution permitted to be openly whipped, from which punishment they were exempt. At the various elections this entirely uneducated caste was like a shuttlecock in the hands of the ambitious oligarchy; they were always open to bribery, it was one of their greatest vices. The people in France are won by crosses and ribbons, in England by heavy gold; but in Hungary a few casks of wine and a little pocket money were sufficient. The lords often ruined each other at these elections; each tried to surpass the other in the grandeur of their pageants, hoping thus to captivate the senses of the electors. The commoner wondered why the great lords cared so much about an office that only lasted three years,

* This was the name given to the lowest class of nobles.

and after all must give them a great deal more trouble than pleasure. But, alas, his wonder was but a short-lived one, for he soon discovered that these officials demanded interest and compound interest of him, who had had no part or interest in the election. The Government is reproached with having introduced this bribery and corruption *en gros*, and the Opposition, which made use of the same vicious means, excused itself by saying that it was compelled to adopt it as a weapon of defence. But the "statesphilosopher" must hold such a principle as dishonourable, and condemn it even if it is practised for a seeming good.

These, then, were the component parts of the Hungarian constitution! the peasant nobility, the landed nobility, the magnates and the prelates; these were the 500,000 souls that inhabited the 6000 German square miles, ruling over the rest of the population, which amounted to 14,000,000 souls, monopolizing not only all the dignities and offices of State, but justice, freedom, riches, and power. Why, then, are you surprised at the neglect of intellectual and material cultivation? Why are you surprised at the depravity and voluptuousness which sometimes almost exceeded that of the French Court in the reign of Louis XV. The constitution was a body without a soul, a brilliant show as far as regarded words, but it was without the fire of life, without producing-power for the majority: the rights that it bestowed were unjust, the freedom that it boasted of was nothing more nor less than the freedom to make slaves; the commoner was in a worse condition than he who sighed under the despotism of the Turkish Sultan. The majesty of the king was a mere sound signifying nothing; he had neither the power to do good or suppress evil. It was the Magnates which were entrusted with the power of sovereignty, and against them there was no appeal; when their *privileges* were not sufficient to carry their will through, they employed *force*. Each power in the State was paralysed by the other,—the king by the nobles, the nobles by the unsympathising masses, the masses by the king and nobles. The law was of the most arbitrary description, a continual mockery of justice. The lawgiver was at the same time judge and executioner, and the people a people without a present, without a future, without a name, without a language, without a hope of improvement—a lifeless mass enveloped in the rags of a wretched existence.

Even this lifeless mass was divided into two

castes, viz.: burghers and peasants. The burghers were a good-natured kind of folk that always looked after the profits, however shamefully they were oppressed. They were chiefly engaged in manufactures and commerce, and were the principal inhabitants of the larger towns; by degrees certain territorial privileges were bestowed upon them, which placed them far above the peasants, though they did not put them on an equality with the Bocskoros.

The privileges aroused the animosity of the peasants, and made the union of these two castes impossible. Thus the working classes, the burgher and the peasant, the representatives of the agricultural and physical development of the state, looked upon each other with envious eyes, and hearts full of anger and scorn. Burgher and peasant, the only real power of the State, the kernel of the fruit, were annihilated by the laws, or rather condemned to inactivity. Though the nobles had courts where they were tried by their peers, yet even the word justice was unknown to the burgher and the peasant. But how could it be expected that they should know the meaning of the word when they had never tasted of the fruits of justice? The burgher saw the noble effecting his desires by bribery and despotic oppression, and was it not natural that he should have recourse to the same means as far as he was able?

Honour, justice, and honesty, disappeared by degrees from the great whole; and again the effect was condemned without having regard to the cause. The burghers were divided into trades, and they watched with astonishment and horror the gulf widening between them and the peasant, and, like the snail at the approach of danger, they drew in their horns, and began to look upon him who appeared to meddle with politics as a privileged oppressor. Politics they hated because they were, as they thought, without use and beyond their reach, and because they imagined they were the amusement of those who could practise every kind of injustice without being punished for it; who could contract debts without being obliged to pay them; who might maltreat or make sport of the burgher if he were so inclined. They looked upon politics as a sorcerer's cave, in which poisonous draughts were brewed from the parchment which legalized the levying of taxes, and soldiers, and the limitation of trade; draughts for which they could find no antidote, in spite of their industry and care. What would have been the use of the burgher's having the noblest ideas about the State and society? He would never have been able to carry them out,—not even to communicate them to his fellow burghers, except in the taverns.

And now we have arrived at the lowest grade of the population of Hungary—the peasant. The peasant received blows from all; the prelate, the magnate, the noble, aye even the burgher heaped blows and insults upon the wretched peasant; nothing was done without flogging; from the peasant's cradle to the peasant's grave, his only comfort was the stick. There were regal, ecclesiastical, domestic, patrimonial, criminal, and additional floggings. In fact, the society of Hungary might have been divided into two classes, active and passive, *i.e.* floggers and flogged. The stick was the peasant's right, his education, his property. An old nobleman once made the following remark to a philanthropist who was anxious to abolish flogging: "You might just as well abolish nobility at the same time. What would our prerogatives be worth if the law no longer allowed the peasant to be flogged? You must please to recollect that to flog him is our exceptional privilege." And it was in the hands of such lovers of humanity that the helm of State was placed!

ANSWER II.

You surely must know that in countries where the land is possessed by a privileged aristocracy, this aristocracy generally can find a means to advance the education of the people, and to raise the standard of the native literature; for by elevating the tendencies and ideas of the masses they render the most important services to the State. I think you must yourself confess, that you have not discovered the right remedy for the evils which beset Hungary. The system of the landed proprietors as it existed in Hungary was calculated to strengthen the Government, and force it to adopt liberal institutions. The system of landed property when it is properly taxed, (and the only just tax is the land tax,) enables the Treasury to dispense its means properly; and induces the taxpayer, if not prevented by indolence, to increase the profit of his land by raising its cultivation. Riches create wants, and when these wants are not material and sensual (as was unfortunately the case in Hungary) they are of an intellectual nature: these wants again create authors, thinkers, philosophers, and then statesmen arise, who only can exist where they are able to win the sympathy of a people. If everything had gone on regularly in Hungary a thousand years would have formed a very different sort of society to that which existed in 1848; and the results of a *just* insurrection on the part of a nation physically and intellectually powerful would have been very different to that which you are shortsighted enough to lament.

The principles of the foundation of the Magyar State were false; therefore society, which was formed upon those principles, must also be false. All that tended to curse the land grew here abundantly. All that fed uselessly upon society and oppressed it, was everywhere at hand. Thus, the number of lawyers in Hungary was much larger than in any other country; at the end of the last century they were more numerous than the peasants and tradespeople.* These lawyers, who in 1848 were comparatively just as numerous, were like birds of prey and lived at the expense of the working and possessing classes, and as they were not paid by the State, they were the guiding elements of the revolution. It is impossible to say what confusion of ideas, what depravity, what misery, what dishonour prevailed among these myrmidons of the law. And yet you maintain that "Hungary had not its vitality centred solely in its heart, like

* Benkoe, "Topographia Oppidi Miskolcz. Cassoviæ," 1782 in 4to.

France; it had vitality in each of its members, and was even living without interruption;" but I ask you, what were the results of this life?

Everything that makes a State powerful and durable was parched, withered and dead!

ANSWER III.

IN your letters you also mention the religious condition of Hungary, and your principal object seems to be, to prove how far the Austrian Government has been capable of "Hungariam facere catholicam, Germanam et miseram." If this is the case, I must beg you to inform me as to what the constitution was really capable of effecting? Did the Austrian Government proceed to carry out these terrible plans in a constitutional or anti-constitutional manner? If the latter, where was the power of resistance which of right belonged to the constitution? You must not believe for an instant, that I wish to defend the Austrian Government: according to my political principles a Government is nothing but the efflux of the majority of a people. It is my intention to show you how perverted your conception and representation is, and that you never have taken the trouble to associate the constitutional principles of your country with their application. But a true philosophical perception is that which seeks for elementary principles, in order to prove what must be the effect they produce.

My last Answer has shown how the laws of the constitution of the Magyars created that state of social condition which I have already described; but as the religion of a State has no less influence upon its physical and intellectual development than its laws, I feel compelled to reply to your very vague and superficial remarks upon the Church and Reformation in Hungary, by referring again to history.

In page 20 you say: "Before 1849 the most complete toleration prevailed among the different religious sects, Roman Catholics, Greek Catholics of both Churches, Protestants of both confessions, Unitarians and Jews. This toleration was itself the fruit of our political liberty,"—and then follows shortly after another passage, which I must quote on account of its *truth;* it reads as follows:—" I freely confess, in this lay the great merit of the Roman Catholic clergy; the *richest* and *most* privileged in Europe, but at the same time the *most* tolerant and *most* popular: who lived without isolating themselves from the people, and without hypocritical affectation."

Such are the hyperbolical expressions which

you, as a Protestant, make use of when writing of the Romish clergy, because the political aim, which you hope to obtain by this Machiavellian praise, swims before your obscure vision. You have evidently learnt something of the principles of the richest clergy in Europe. Some States have relied upon the mere outbursts and fancies of the national will, like Rome—and Rome has fallen; others have relied upon their religious administration, like the Egyptians, and the Jews—they disappeared; or like the Turks—and he would be blind who could not see the near approach of their ruin; for the religion of Mahomet is not capable of social development. Hungary has relied solely upon *casuistry in politics*. If religion had not always been subservient to the policy of the State, the true faith would have inspired the Hungarians with a love for freedom, and thus their physical and mental development would have been insured.

But here, again, your liberal constitution was the stumbling-block.

After the disastrous battle of Mohacs, John Zapolya was elected by a part of the nation, assembled at Stuhlweissenburg, to fill the throne rendered vacant by the death of Lewis II. But Ferdinand I. of Austria had just claims to the

ANSWER III.

throne of Hungary, which, according to all old documents, was not an elective, but an hereditary monarchy. The Salic law never existed in Hungary. After the death of Stephen, his sister Gisella was heir to the kingdom, and, through her, the crown descended to her son Peter. Maria, Queen of Naples, sister of Ladislaw IV., maintained her claim to the throne after the death of Andreas III., but she transferred her rights to her son Charles Martel, and from him the crown descended to her grandson Charles Robert. The oracle of the then existing Christendom—the Pope—asserted, before God and man, that "the Hungarian kingdom was not to be obtained by election but by inheritance."* But what did the magnates and nobles care about the law? John Zapolya had a very strong party in the country which carried his election in opposition to the law; and as the Protestants declared generally for the party of the widowed Queen, who wished to place her brother Ferdinand I. on the throne, the first act of Zapolya was to issue an edict against the Lutherans. The new King threatened to confiscate all their estates if they refused to become Roman Catholics; he

* Scripti canonis series aperit Regnum ipsum Hungariæ successionis jure provenit; electionis arbitrio non defertur. Bonifacii viii. Bulla Spectorum Omnium, 30 Jun. 1303.

hoped by this edict to gratify the *very tolerant* priest, Paul Warday, Archbishop of Gran, whom he was anxious to propitiate.

The widowed Queen Maria was extremely attached to the doctrines propagated by Luther. She saw the utter depravity of the Romish clergy, and as a high-minded, intellectual woman she could not look with indifference on the ruin they were bringing on the land. Thuruschwamm, a contemporary of Lewis II, who has written very trustworthy chronicles, has preserved but too true a picture of the clergy of those times. I will quote his own words: " For many years the bishops and clergy have ruined Hungary. They have ever anxiously sought all high offices at court, and have striven to become councillors, chancellors, treasurers, and governors. I have seen Peter, Bishop of Wesprim, Ban, *i.e.*, Governor of Dalmatia, Croatia, and Bosnia. Look at Bishop Falkanus! his dictatorial sway has emptied the royal coffers; he not only governs the land, but the king, who is actually compelled to submit to him and depend upon him."*

The Reformation, which was the most glorious fruit of German intellect, spread in a most remarkable manner in Hungary. The means chosen

* John Ribinyi, Memor. Aug. Conf. Part. page 17.

by Providence were at the same time the most extraordinary and the most admirable. Rough and thoughtless German soldiers, who came to defend Hungary from the Turks, were the first to make known the doctrines of Luther. Luther's hymns, the Psalms in the German language, and last, but not least, his translation of the New Testament, elevated and purified the masses; crowds of Germans and Hungarians were converted to the reformed faith. The Queen Maria, who was not so weak as her consort, encouraged the Reformation for the sake of morality. This high-minded princess warned her brother Charles not to allow the priests to deceive him at the Diet at Augsburg, as they had already deceived her husband. Johann Henkel, a friend of Erasmus, preached the word of God in her court, and Luther himself corresponded with her. In one of his letters, in which he enclosed four psalms that he had translated from the original on purpose for her consolation, he writes: "I have seen with great pleasure that you are a friend of the Gospel." But her husband, as well as his successor, did not follow her bright example. Excited by the intolerant Magyar prelates, they ordered the Bibles to be publicly burnt by the hangman.* Luther's writ-

* See the Oedenburg City Records of Father Visper, 1525.

ings were taken from the burgher by force. The myrmidons of the law forced an entrance into the houses of the burgher and peasant, and destroyed every trace of the new doctrines. The magnates showed a spirit of tolerance of a most peculiar description, for, at a Diet that was held upon the Rakoscher heath, on the 15th of August, 1524, at which the King and Archbishop presided, they decreed that "All Lutherans shall be rooted out of the land; and wherever they may be found, either by clergy or layman, they are to be seized and burnt."* Where, then, was the wonderful power of your liberal constitution, which, you maintain, converted every house into a castle.

The Romish prelates were not distinguished by any great firmness of character, for Paul Warday, Archbishop of Gran, solemnly crowned Ferdinand of Austria King of Hungary at Stuhlweissenburg, just twelve months after he had assisted at the coronation of Johann von Zapolya, by whom he was made primate of the kingdom.

Where the dignitaries of Church and State esteem oaths and laws thus lightly, it is impossible for the nation to prosper. Johann Zapolya endeavoured to retain the throne by persecuting

* Cæsar Baronius, Annal 1525. Article 4, anni 1525.

the Lutherans and paying court to the Turks; but the Turkish Pasha showed a higher sense of justice than this Oligarch of Hungary, for, by the mouth of his ambassador, he said: "Si Ferdinandus aliam justitiam non haberet, nisi eam, quia sororem habet Regis Ludovici, potius ejus justitia apud Deum est, quam tui Domini (Zapolyæ).*

But in spite of this Zapolya's ambition was not satisfied. Of what value was faith or Christianity in his eyes? One day he condemned the Pastor Nicolai and a schoolmaster to the stake, because "they had refused the *Virgin Mary* her due honour;" the next this severe Christian threw himself humbly at the feet of the Sultan Solyman, who promised "to look upon this most Christian King's fortune as his own." And he kept his word —like a heathen. He came to Zapolya's assistance. Ferdinand of Austria was defeated, and the country laid waste as far as Vienna; but there the Turkish ally of the Christian Zapolya met with the most determined resistance on the part of the *German* burghers and students. As soon as fortune forsook his banners Zapolya was abandoned both by his heathen and Christian allies; the prelates setting

* Hieronym. Lasky Hist. arcan. Legation, ap. *Bel*, Monum. Decad. I. page 167.

thus the most disgraceful example by their mean and wavering conduct.

Paul Warday, as soon as he saw Ferdinand compelled to seek his safety in flight, had endeavoured to fasten himself on to the party favourable to the pretensions of Zapolya, and at the intercession of Solyman he was again permitted to kiss the hand of the usurper, and defended the castle of Gran against the royal troops. In Croatia a few men who remained faithful to the Austrian killed Simon Erdödy, bishop of Agram, and robbed him of his treasure, which the Sultan had permitted him to take with him as a reward for his treachery to his king and his religion. It was in vain that Zapolya beheaded the followers of the rightful king;[*] it was impossible for him to retain his hold on the throne. The Sultan once more invested Zapolya with the kingdom of Hungary, and swore solemnly that he would never forsake him under any circumstances, "*even if it were to cost him his own land;*" after which he withdrew from Hungary, taking with him *sixty thousand* men and women as serfs and prisoners, most of whom were Hungarians. During the progress of these events, the Christian vassal

[*] Stephen Polthurnyánzky at Dunajecz. See Fessler, Vol. VI., p. 346.

of the Osman wrote to the Austrians much the same sort of letters as those with which you have honoured Mr. Cobden, in which he accused Ferdinand I. of having brought so much misery upon the country, and entreated them, even threateningly, for the sake of Christendom (what mockery!) to try and induce him to adopt more peaceable intentions towards Hungary.*

Will you be kind enough to point out any other kingdom in the world, where the natives have been guilty of such frightful treacheries to their king and their religion, to civilization and the poorer classes of their fellow-countrymen? Did you ever hear of any other political party that allied itself to the deadliest foes of Christendom at the same time that it endeavoured to extirpate heresy with fire and sword? When and where have you ever read of a Tory or Whig who would have allowed the Turks to carry 60,000 Christians into slavery!—who would have allowed 60,000 Christians to be sacrificed body and soul? And do you think that the ruling Spirit of the Universe will allow a nation to commit such horrible crimes with impunity?

* See Fessler's Geschichte der Ungern, Vol. VI., p. 438. Also Liter. Joannis Zapol., ad Stat. et Ord. Austriæ ap. Pray Epist. Proc., P. I., page 348.

If you wish to excite sympathy, you must draw a veil over the past, or mark it as the black book of barbarism up to modern times,—yes, even up to the present day.

But I must not interrupt the thread of history by untimely remarks.

The Roman Catholic Kings of Hungary, whom you represent as the enemies of Protestantism, committed their most cruel persecutions only with the help of the Magyar constitution, and they were never more in accordance with it, than when they persecuted both Lutherans and Calvinists.

You say, page 102, "that the Emperor of Austria has only given back to the Hungarian Protestants the same thoroughly democratic constitution which was given to them at Vienna in 1606, at Lintz 1645, and at Strathmar-Németi in 1711." And, in imitation of Zapolya, you add: "Thus all that is liberal and good in this document belongs purely and simply to Hungary; what is bad and Jesuitical—and there is plenty of that—is of Austrian origin." But you forget to make us acquainted with what it is, that is bad and Jesuitical, and you only allow them to be right, who reject this thoroughly democratic constitution merely because it is imposed on them by Austria.

You must, however, allow me to point out who were the men who supported the Reformation, and who were those, who fed the dark passions of the age that existed in the heart of the Roman Catholic kings and emperors, exciting them to a mad fanaticism. We shall behold a long and brilliant line of apostate magnates, we shall see how the Roman Catholic kings of Hungary had to struggle with their Magyar bishops, in order to protect their Protestant subjects from the most bloody persecutions.

As soon as Ferdinand I. had made peace with Zapolya, he, contrary to the most urgent request of bishops Frater, Statitius, and Frangepan, refused to allow the Protestant preachers, Devay and Szentai, to be arrested and treated as heretics; but he commanded a public discussion to be held on religious matters. This frightened the bishops pretty considerably, more especially as Ferdinand chose two remarkably honest umpires, Dr. Adrian, vicar of Stuhlweissenburg, and Martin Kalmentsi, the rector of the school. The discussion proceeded, and the report of it given by the umpires was, that Szentai had proved all his assertions by the Scriptures; and although George Frater, bishop of Grosswardein, appeared before the king, and heaped reproaches upon him in the name of the other bishops, prelates, and monks, even threatening him with the Pope's displeasure, yet Ferdinand remained unmoved, and answered the insolent prelate with dignity and firmness. "I will put no man to death until he has been proved guilty of a capital crime. Bring forward your charge, and he shall be judged according to the law." The bishop's rage increased, when the King added "It does not become my royal dignity to punish innocence;" and almost mad with passion the priest exclaimed: "If your Majesty will not grant our request, we shall find *other remedies* to free us from this vulture!"

On the same evening the humane King gave audience to Stephen Szentai. After he had conversed a long time with the noble preacher about the truths of the Scriptures, he gave vent to the following melancholy speech: "My dear brother Stephen, if we adhere to these doctrines you and I are lost; meantime we must commit our cause to God, who alone knows what is best. You must, however, leave the country, or the princes will imprison and condemn you to death, and I could only endanger myself without being able to deliver you." These words of the king utterly condemn your admirable constitution! How can you lay all the misery of the country exclusively to the kings' account, when the kings themselves were without power or authority.

During a long reign of thirty-five years, which was one continual struggle with the Turks and his own subjects, it is scarcely possible to reproach the King, under whom the Reformation first began to spread in Hungary, with one voluntary act of malicious cruelty. In vain they hoped to throw suspicion upon the confession of faith of the five cities, known also under the name of "Pentapolitan;" but the King apprized himself of their tenets, and then permitted them freely to practise their religion. When he was old, his strength worn out by constant toil, and his mental powers enfeebled, he allowed a Jesuit, who was pressed upon him by the Pope, to enter his kingdom and endeavour to eradicate the reformed doctrines. When we take into consideration that this prince was educated at the court of Spain, that he was a brother of the Emperor Charles, who was not particularly tolerant in religious matters; when we recollect that the court of Rome held the Emperor and King in the meanest subjection; that Luther's doctrines were described as inimical to any form of government; that in Hungary the Reformation was actually looked upon as a mere political conspiracy; when, in addition to all this, and the spirit of the times, we call to mind the condition of society, and the position of the Roman Emperor with regard to the church, we must indeed be blinded by partiality if we condemn Ferdinand I. for any one act of his long reign. Statesmen when they sit in judgment upon a nation's past, can only do it truthfully by examining into the detailed circumstances of events, their effects, and the causes from which these effects arose.

After the death of Ferdinand, Maximilian I. ascended the throne. If there ever existed a prince who possessed all the good qualities of a great king, it was this noble and enlightened monarch. Archbishop Olah, a Magyar, tried every possible means to induce the Emperor to adopt severe measures against the Lutherans; but his efforts were not crowned with success. The first command that Maximilian issued, was, that the archbishop was not to molest the Protestants, but to take care that he did not destroy more, by his untimely zeal, than he was capable of restoring.* The most zealous supporter of Protestantism was

* Ribinyi Mem. Mica Burg. MS.

the German Imperial Commander-General of the Forces, Lazarus Schwend.

Maximilian carried his ideas of reform so far, that he hoped to abolish celibacy among the clergy in his dominions. He opposed every religious persecution, as he was convinced that the new creed would not prevent the burghers fulfilling their duties to the State.

Upon all this the Romish clergy looked with jealous eyes. They envied the religious liberties of the Protestants, and, by the misrepresentation of facts, they endeavoured to persuade Maximilian to adopt harsher measures. In spite of their opposition the utmost excitement prevailed, and found vent everywhere in the greatest variety of creeds. This deviation from the true path, and an unbridled extravagance of opinion, split the reformers into parties, some of which joined the Arians, others the Socinians; and this division of interests led to a speedy reaction.

The Magyar Gregorius Bornesmissza, Bishop of Csanad, undertook to make the twenty-four German Zipser towns, which he called "his towns," to acknowledge the error of their ways, and to bring them again within the pale of the Romish Church. The intellect of the Hungarian Protestants was centred in the Germans. The first rays of the purer doctrine were brought into Hungary by German cavalry soldiers; and the talented young students, who wished to devote themselves to the propagation of the Word of God, were sent to pursue their studies at Gratz, Silesia, and Wittenberg; the latter university was more generally chosen. This emigration of Hungarian students of the Protestant confession was, until lately, always permitted. Many a man whose name sounds well in the annals of Hungarian literature, completed his studies in Germany, and has to thank the language of universal knowledge for every ray of profound reflection.

In spite of all intrigues; in spite of the rebellion of Bocskay, and the bloody example which the French king, Charles IX., set to all orthodox Romanists; in spite of the suspicions of reckless priests, who accused Protestantism of every reform which was in accordance with the spirit of the age, though Protestantism, in its turn, was but the child of a time when the art of printing, the invention of gunpowder, the discovery of America, the stirling ideas of the great thinkers of England and Germany, introduced a new era in the development of the human race;—in spite of priestly fanaticism, Maximilian remained true to his tolerant principles. After the death of Cithardus, a man named Martin Eisengrün, a Protestant apostate, was appointed court preacher. In the first sermon that he delivered before the Emperor he attacked the liberty of the Protestants, in consequence of which the Emperor deprived him of his post, and sent him to the monastery of Dettingen, in Bavaria. It is a well-known fact that a great many of the dignitaries of the State,—even ambassadors at the court of Rome,—were sometimes Protestants: therefore, up to that time, your complaints are totally without foundation.

But suddenly the scene changes; Rudolph ascends the throne. Rudolph, the son of a bigoted Spanish mother, was educated by Jesuits; he was hardly twelve years old when he was sent to Spain, to the court of the gloomy and suspicious Philip II, who endeavoured to stay the spirit of progress by the executioner's axe of the Duke of Alva, and the faggots of the Grand Inquisitor, Torquemada. It was here that Rudolph learned to esteem the Romish Church above everything; a Church which presumed to command the sun to stand still—to direct the flow of the thoughts of man. Unfortunately, it is possible for a man to be religious,—yes, even moral,—and yet commit the most dreadful deeds in consequence of his mistaken religious views. When the ruling spirit of intellectual consciousness and self-denial is wanting, and the outward form consumes the spirit of true religion, it is then that religion becomes the scourge of mankind. At the same time, it is but in the course of nature that mankind should go through certain phases in its religious development, as well as that of its political existence.

It is well for Hungary that neither a Bloody Mary, nor a Charles IX., nor a Philip II., ever held its sceptre. If Rudolph's mind had not been occupied with the arts and sciences of his times, such as astrology, alchemy, and painting, he would, most probably, have reigned with the same justice and tolerance as his father. He was, however, almost always locked up in his laboratory, trying to discover that mysterious power which holds the universe together in its inmost sphere. He sought for cement in matter, and forgot the Eternal Spirit. He spent millions in searching for the "philosopher's stone;" but that this stone lay hidden in a pure heart and unfettered mind, he, like many another monarch, never imagined even in his wildest dreams. Rudolph would have preferred not being troubled at all with the toils of government. Nothing roused his anger so much as to be called away from his retorts and phials, his primary elements, his *ovum philosophicum*, his red lion, or his white lily.* The monarch was surrounded by astrologers, who pampered his weakness, or who really believed in the theories of their age,—who can be free from them?—by alchemists, who stole his gold by handfuls in order to teach him to make silver; by artists, who excited his imagination and indulged his caprice with a view to their own interests; and, lastly, by wanton frivolous mistresses, who cared for nothing but his money. Who then can wonder at the Jesuits gaining the ascendancy over the minds of the people, and inciting them against the reformed doctrines? Who can be surprised at these Jesuits, at last, being able to move the Emperor-king to adopt more severe measures against the followers of the new religion? But it was Gregorius Bornemissza, Bishop of Gross-Wardein, and George Draskovitch, Archbishop of Kalocsa, and *not the King himself*, who opposed the Protestants with all the terrors in their power. They

* Technical terms used by alchemists.

seized every opportunity to persecute the Reformers; they even took advantage of the occasion which the introduction of the Gregorian calendar offered to prosecute their bloody intentions. Although this calendar was much more correct in its calculations than the Julian, yet the fanatical zeal of the Protestants would not allow them to acknowledge it, because it came from Rome.

It was Draskovitch, and not King Rudolph, who, in the bitterest spirit of persecution, brought the Jesuits into the kingdom of Hungary. On the contrary, it was an Austrian Emperor who expelled this order from his kingdom; but he fell a sacrifice to his liberalism. His life was a brilliant example to all; but, alas, much too short! Pope Sixtus V. knew quite well on whom to bestow his rewards, and a cardinal's hat was destined to cover the narrow head of Draskovitch. It was the Roman general, Barbiano, and no German, who, with the assistance of three Magyar bishops, robbed the Protestants of Kaschau of their churches, expelled the German pastors from the country, endeavoured to convert the unhappy people by the edge of the sword, and even forbade them to receive the Lord's supper. Rudolph II., like Charles II. of England, was exactly the man under whom it would have been possible for the nation to develope itself morally and intellectually; but the miserable family feuds of the Bathorys and Bocskays, the Bethlens and Drugets, did not permit this. Once more the land was exposed to the struggles of factions, and the miseries of famine, which were soon followed by the most cruel persecutions of the Protestants, and a most sanguinary rebellion, which brought about a second alliance between the pious and liberal Christians, and the Turks under the Grand Vizier Mahomet, who willingly poured his plundering troops into the land, at the bidding of those, who wished it to be supposed, that they were struggling for religious freedom. And again the heathen and Christian fraternize, and we see the horrible spectacle of a Christian Prince receiving his kingdom at the hands of a Turkish Grand Vizier.*

The unequivocal manner in which the Magyars always showed their dislike to Austria,—their anxiety to seize every opportunity of calling in the Turks, French, Poles, and Italians to help them against Austria,—was not calculated to create a mutual confidence between monarch and people,

* Bocskay. See Feszler's Geschichte der Ungern. Vol. VII., p. 588.

—people, taken in the sense accepted by the Magyar constitution; that is to say, with the exception of the millions of tax-paying burghers and peasants. In spite of all intrigues, the Peace of Vienna was concluded, on the 23rd of June, 1606, and the first legal document which granted the Protestants religious liberty was issued.

Rudolph was succeeded by Matthias, who was much more liberally disposed; and again two Magyars particularly distinguished themselves in his reign, by their bitter and revengeful animosity against the Protestants,—trying to prevent the abolition of the 22nd Article, which had been inserted by the Jesuits and Catholic prelates, in opposition to all legal right, at the diet held in Presburg, 1604.

This Article decreed, "that, under severe penalties no complaint against religious matters was to be brought before the Diet. It described the Protestant religion as an innovation, and spoke of it in terms of the greatest contempt. It required all the laws enacted against dissent from the Church of Rome (consequently the burning at the stake) to be observed; and it commanded the King to consider it his solemn and responsible duty to spread the Roman Catholic religion, and root out all sects and heresies."*

The abolition of this Article was, of course, a question of life and death to Protestantism in Hungary; but political reasons induced Matthias to annul it. As soon as the Hungarian Protestants began to avail themselves of their legal rights,— which secured to the elders, ministers, and superintendents of each confession full authority over the members of their own Church,—the Cardinal Archbishop Forgács opposed the law, even in defiance of the King, whom he threatened with excommunication in such a determined manner, that he almost incurred the penalty of high treason. He considered that if the Protestants ventured to choose their own superintendents,—who were again empowered to ordain their own clergy, —that they broke the laws of the land, and acted contrary to *religious liberty!* and he accused all Protestants of perjury, and cursed them as heretics.† But the Magyar Cardinal Peter Pazman was still more dangerous to the Protestant

* Rudolphi Reg. Decret. XV. Art. XXII., in Corp. Jur. Hung. T. I., p. 637.
† This document is dated from "Our Archiepiscopal Court at Presburg, April 17th, 1610," and was first published by means of a nail on the church door of St. Martin's. Hist. Dipl. pp. 27—29.

cause than this furious prelate. His secret intrigues obliged the liberal Matthias to abdicate in favour of Ferdinand II.

Not Hungary alone, but the whole of Europe, was, at this time, disturbed by the last desperate efforts of the Romish court. For thirty years, the most sanguinary war recorded in the annals of history desolated Germany; but the lesser numbers were victorious, not only over the overwhelming power of Tilly, but over the military genius of Wallenstein; and why? Because no meaner purpose alloyed the enthusiasm of the Germans; no political or national interests, and no wish for the exclusive privileges of caste, were mixed up with the desire to secure perfect freedom to each individual to settle all religious matters between himself and his Creator. The Germans trusted in the justice of their cause. It was for the purity of their faith that they hoped, fought, and died. But, because the Magyars had other interests at heart, they did not hesitate, even as Protestants, to throw themselves at the feet of the bitterest foes of Christendom; they hesitated not, at the expense of faith and honour, to submit to the barbarous Turks, because, by so doing, they hoped to promote their own *selfish* purposes.

When Ferdinand II. ascended the throne, the country was torn by political as well as religious factions. Rudolph II. had been educated in the dark errors of the Romish Church; but it had never been the intention of those who instructed him, to educate him as an instrument of vengeance, as an inexorable persecutor of the daily increasing doctrines of Reform. This, however, had been the fate of Ferdinand II.; as a boy he had taken a most solemn oath that he would "extirpate the heretics," at whatever cost to himself. He undertook various pilgrimages to Loretto, to implore the protection of the "Queen of Heaven." Accompanied and surrounded by Jesuits, he visited the Pope, and besought his blessing on his horrible undertaking. On a second pilgrimage to some miraculous picture, which he undertook in his fortieth year, he fancied he heard a voice, accompanied by a dreadful storm that shook the gothic building to its foundations, speak these encouraging words: "Ferdinand, I will not forsake thee."

This shows us what means were employed to excite the imagination of this Emperor-king. Ferdinand was not without character, and for this reason he became a fearful instrument in the hands of those who misused his powers. But who were these men who raged thus furiously in Hungary, who ought to have been able to resist any unjust oppression on the part of the King of this admirable constitution,—"this Palladium of liberties?" They were Magyars! This terrible Pazman, who had once been a Lutheran, but abjured the faith of his fathers,—who became a Jesuit and the most cruel persecutor of those who had formerly been his fellow-believers,—this noble prince of the church was not ashamed to say, "I would rather see my villages forsaken and lying waste, than that a single church for the benefit of Protestant subjects should rear its head on my estates."*

Pazman was a worthy associate of the Magyar Count Stephen Palfy, who erected gallows on his territory, and made known his intention of hanging every Protestant preacher that should venture to set foot in his estates. You must be fully aware that these and similar threats, on the part of the Romish lords, led to equal cruelties on the part of the Protestants. Gabriel Bethlen having closed an alliance with the followers of Mahomet *for the protection* of the Gospel, and taken Kaschau (a town in Upper Hungary,) hung the

* Engel, Geschichte der Ungern, Vol. IV. page 398.

ANSWER III. 79

Jesuits Stephan Pongracz, Melchior Grodetzky, and the Canon Marcus Crisinius of Gran. The tolerance of the Hungarian Romanists and Protestants, of which you boast so much, is therefore but a delusion of your own.

Again nothing but desolation, persecution, murder and death, stares us in the face. Nicolaus Eszterhazy, Palatine of Hungary, also an apostate Lutheran, must now be placed with Pazman and Palfy, at the head of the persecutors of progress and religious liberty. The Protestant Gabriel Bethlen allied himself once more with the Turks, and now nothing but a grey monotony passes before the historian's eye, a repetition of the events under Zapolya and Bocskay takes place under Gabriel Bethlen. Nothing has progressed since Zapolya's time (*i. e.* for nearly a century) but perfidy and treachery. The stern s.phist Pazman, assisted by Ferdinand II., who liberally rewarded all apostates, succeeded in converting forty of the principal Magyar families to Romanism. It is well known that Adam Batthyány and Adam Thurzo from this period persecuted the Protestants "*ad majorem Mariæ gloriam,*"* to such an extent that Cardinal Klesel, Archbishop of

* Hist. Reform. p. 376.

Vienna, exhorted them to be more indulgent and tolerant, but the answer he received from the Emperor was, "*Malo regnum desolatum quam damnatum.*" *

But while the Magyar magnates allowed themselves to be converted, the German clergy of the twenty-four "Zipser towns" remained faithful to the Reformed Church, for which contumacy Cardinal Pazman punished them with excommunication.

Ferdinand III., who while carrying on war in Germany was threatened by the Turks in Hungary, was glad enough to consent to all demands for religious freedom; but soon after the death of Pazman, another apostate, the Magyar Bishop of Erlau, Emerich Losy, in conjunction with the apostate Adam Thurzo turned his whole attention to the persecution of the Protestants. Again a revolution broke out under George Rakotzy, and again they asked the protection of the Turks and sought the alliance of France and Sweden. But while the Swedes were pressing forward and the Turks delayed their arrival, the Magyar zealots under Count Francis Révay and the Archbishop Lippay expelled and persecuted the pastors of all

* "I would rather have a desolate than an accursed kingdom."

confessions with inexorable cruelty. In this dire necessity George Rakotzky gave up his Swedish alliance for the promise of two counties; and the Peace of Linz, which restored to the Protestants their rights and liberties, was closed December 16th, 1645.

And what did the Magyar Roman Catholic clergy do? They submitted humbly to the Romish Court, and showed themselves so thoroughly indifferent to their duties to King and country, that instead of convoking the Diet within three months after the peace, according to the King's promise, they postponed it for ten months. At last the Diet was convoked and the Romish clergy entered their protest against the peace, and for months they prevented its conditions being put into execution, by endeavouring to upset its validity. The Palatine Draskovich and Archbishop Lippay behaved in a most unseemly manner at the Diet; the former drew his sword and swore to defend the Jesuits with his life, and the language of the Archbishop became so violent, that he was threatened with dismissal from office.

What has been presented to our view in the course of this historical sketch? Have we seen the different religious parties treating each other better in Hungary than in any other country, where Romanism and Protestantism opposed each other, either in intellectual controversy or upon the field of battle? The undeveloped state of civilization was the cause of this hostility; we are not surprised that it existed, but we are surprised that you should wish to make the world believe that every idea of persecution in Hungary originated with the German government. It plainly shows that the art of distorting facts is rooted, as of old, in the Magyar diplomatists and statesmen; they were and are ever ready to assert and misrepresent, confessing openly, "We know it is not true, but that does not signify, if we can only injure Austria and the Germans."

The times are past and gone when it was possible to make a fortune by the tricks of a pettifogger and sophistical reasoning, or when a Machiavelli was permitted for the sake of his country to publish absolutistic ideas to conceal his republican thoughts. Fortunately those times exist no longer! You must surely perceive that your apostle of national freedom * does not succeed in deluding the world by his dispatches in the style of Talleyrand. It is this double tongued

* Louis Napoleon.

immorality which will cause this man's ruin, and call all Europe to arms to destroy his immoral faithlessness, which is the destructive element in the normal development of European nations. Truth must be our guide when we wish to throw light upon a nation's past. Truth must inspire us when we speak of its present existence; thus only will it be possible to connect the events of the past, and only thus can we contemplate the history of a single nation with regard to the progressive development of mankind at large.

You must be kind enough to permit me to pass over hastily the horrible reign of Leopold I.,— yes, even that of the celebrated Maria Theresia. Under both governments the Protestants were exposed to the persecutions of the fanatical Romanists. But why? Because the oppressed Magyar Protestants, headed by Tököly and Rakotzy, sought the alliance of the Turks. They summoned the heathen into the land to enable them to brave their legitimate lord and king, and compel him to yield to their demands. Who can be surprised at the King allowing himself to be persuaded by the Magyar zealots to adopt measures at which he himself would have shuddered. Was it not Prince Paul Esterhazy who endeavoured to convert his Protestant subjects by means of his dragoons? This noble Prince imitated, in his small way, the deeds of Louis le Grand; in whose reign the noble word "dragonade" first came into use.*

But the oligarch, Franz Nadasdy, the Chief Justice of the kingdom, made even a yet more shameful havoc among the Protestants. He attacked peasants like a common highwayman; he placed sentinels on the road, to watch for the Protestants going to church; and, as soon as they appeared, men and women were stripped of their clothing, and sent home naked.† Thus did this Magyar magnate show his contempt of all human laws, and sin against every feeling of decency. What is to be expected of the masses, when the CHIEF JUSTICE is guilty of such outrages?

Again we see the magnates setting the lower classes the worst of examples: instead of the Chief Justice being the bulwark of right, the protector of the laws,—which, in consequence of the Peace of Linz, forbade this dreadful persecution of the Protestants,—we see him setting the example of the most depraved disobedience. No wonder that

* See Trench, "On the Study of Words," p. 129.
† "History of the Protestant Church in Hungary." From the German, by the Rev. J. Craig, D.D., p. 172.

this same man, not long after, closed his ignominious life on the scaffold, as a traitor to his king.

I must be here allowed to say a few words about the confusion that existed in Hungary, with regard to the responsibility of the king. The king is only the impersonation of the highest authority in a government; he is, and must be, not only irresponsible but inviolable. He represents the ideal *unity in the State.* The person of the king may change, but the idea he represents is always the same. There can be no doubt that, of all forms of government which have yet been tried, the monarchical is the best. This form is, however, only possible where the people have learnt not to confuse the head of the State either with the government or his councillors. But when it is the sole aim of Conservatives and Liberals to rid themselves of the head of the State, the country is continually, either actively or passively, in rebellion, and improvement must, therefore, be impossible. This was formerly the case in Scotland, but particularly in Ireland, and it has been the case in Hungary for the last three centuries. The Germans were often accused, in Hungary, of acting in everything from fixed and universal principles *à priori.* This may have prevented a rapid political development; but it strengthens the individual, and, at certain periods, rules the actions of a whole nation. The words, "cultivation" and "humanity" have ever found an echo in the breasts of the masses in Germany; and how much more elevated are these sentiments, than those narrow, exclusive feelings of nationality, that are rooted in the fifteen different races* under Austrian government, every one of which would like to form a nation for itself, with a special government, without considering either their geographical position, the resources of their finances and industry, their social relations to the surrounding States, but only the enthusiastic dreams of the different national leaders. It is not only the European individual, but European mankind, that daily becomes more philosophical. We ever desire to abandon isolated trivialities, and throw ourselves into the arms of that which is great and universal. First comes the patriarchal relation of families; then the small States behold the light of day; lastly, the grand brotherhood of men who think alike expands into being.

In order to form a nation, that nation must not

* Germans, Bohemians, Moravians, Poles, Servians, Wends, Croats, Slaves, Italians, Wallacs, Ruthenians, Magyars, Armenians, Frenchmen, and Friaulians.

be numerically superior to its neighbouring states, but it must stand *intellectually* above the surrounding countries.

It is not enough that the Celts and the Britons (the present inhabitants of Wales) are the oldest possessors of the English soil, or that the Normans once upon a time vanquished the country. Though the Welsh may have their own particular language, and their heroes and a few romantic legends, still they will never lord it over the inhabitants of England. And why? Because England can boast of a Bacon, Newton, Locke, Hume, Hamilton, Buckle, and Mill. And the Germans occupy the same position, with regard to the other petty nationalities living in the German and Austrian territories, as the English do with regard to the Welsh and Irish. A nation which could bring forth an Alexander von Humboldt will not and cannot allow either Bohemians or Magyars, Ruthenians or Servians, to rule over it.

The Germans, who were more humane and tolerant than any other nation, had at the expense of their own freedom and political development, allowed the small national parasites, who lived upon German intellect, to quarrel and fight up to the time of which we speak. But the moment is at hand which must show where the *centre of gravity of middle-European civilization* is situated. Germany, in spite of all concordats, had never thrown the gauntlet of intolerance at religious freedom with that obstinacy which distinguished almost every other nation of Europe; nor was this done in Hungary when ruled by Germans.

The spirit of a Lessing and Herder hovered over the Emperor Joseph II., when he issued his Tolerance-edict. And how was he rewarded for his noble endeavours? Freedom, national greatness, progress and cultivation were sacrificed to the predilection for institutions, which oppressed the people, suffocated every aspiration for political grandeur, opposed progress, and postponed all cultivation for an indefinite period.

You complain, that though Joseph II. wished to do good, he made use of bad means. If your opinion were not that of numberless so-called local statesmen, it would not be worthy of refutation. John Stuart Mill, one of the greatest philosophers and political economists of England, says very clearly: "The early difficulties of spontaneous progress are so great, that there is seldom any choice of means for overcoming them; and a ruler, full of the spirit of improvement, is war-

ranted in the use of any expedients that will attain an end perhaps otherwise unattainable."*
And this certainly is the case. What would England have been without Elizabeth, without Cromwell, without William of Orange?

That the spirit of progress now exists in Austria,—that it has made gigantic steps during the last century, not only towards commercial but intellectual development,—is simply owing to the powerful influence of the greatest monarch that ever graced a throne. You boast of the tolerance of the clergy in general; but I assert that the clergy of every confession first learned tolerance of an Austrian emperor,—of an emperor who commanded the lampoons of which he was the subject to be nailed lower down, so that his people might be better able to read them! These few words must give you some idea of the immeasurable greatness of this monarch. Joseph II., a giant in intellect, at least a century in advance of his time,—in spite of the Magyar constitution, endeavoured to form an *united government*. If he had been tyrannical, like Elizabeth, perhaps he would have attained his object; for I can but agree with Mill, who says, "Liberty, as a prin-

* John Stuart Mill, "On Liberty," p. 23.

ciple, has no application to any state of things anterior to the time when mankind has become capable of being improved by free and equal discussion. Until then, there is nothing for them but implicit obedience to an Akbar or a Charlemagne,—if they are so fortunate as to find one."*

If the Austrian people would have acknowledged these principles as right and acted up to them, they would now have been free. Unfortunately Joseph II. lived too short a time to be able to form a compact whole of the states under his sway. His successors, particularly Francis I. and his minister Prince Metternich, followed out the system of territorial division and political separation; by making exclusive concessions to each of the small nationalities, who, not civilized enough, employed them to cultivate their mutual animosity and hatred.

Do you believe that the sanguinary strife, at which you seem so surprised, that existed between the nationalities,—a feud which, among the Magyars, descended from father to son,—† do you

---

* John Stuart Mill, "On Liberty," p. 23.
† You cannot so entirely have forgotten your own language, as not to be able to remember what the Magyar used to say of the Slave: "Tót nem ember, kása nem étel," the Slave is no more a

believe that this hatred would have been possible, if the Magyars had been capable of discussing political matters openly and quietly? And notwithstanding the tolerance which you so much admire, you must know that they are still incapable of discussing politics freely.*

Mill's opinion, which I have quoted above, cannot be turned about to suit convenience, as facts have ever been in Hungary. The Magyars who tried to play the part of Akbar and Charlemagne, fancied that the other nationalities must necessarily bend to their will; but Akbars and Charlemagnes must be intellectually superior to the masses, or even tolerance becomes useless!

human being, than porridge is food; or that when the Magyar spoke of a Servian, he mentioned him very energetically, as, " Ebadta Rácza," Dog-given Raiz, each word being a bitter insult to the Servian; and when a German was mentioned, it was as a "(D―― m) a Sváb lelkét," D――d (I can find no worthy substitute for the far more disgraceful Magyar word) Swabian soul. These colloquial insults say more for the dreadful social condition of Hungary than all your letters put together. "Words quite as often, and as effectually, embody facts of history, or convictions of the moral common sense, as of the imagination or passion of men."—Trench, "On the Study of Words." p. 5.

* There are many facts that I might adduce, in corroboration of this statement; I will content myself with one which justly excited the indignation of the English Press:—Not long ago, three *students*, well-armed, entered, at midnight, the private dwelling of an editor of a newspaper, at Pesth, with the open intention of revenging themselves upon him for his political principles. Not finding him at home, they contented themselves with robbing him of his papers.

ANSWER IV.

There can be nothing accidental in the historical development of a nation, nothing but what has grown out of circumstances. Everywhere we meet with effects that must necessarily have arisen from causes that have once existed. Now that I have historically proved that your assertion respecting the tolerance of the various religious parties in Hungary is but an unfounded hypothesis; I will endeavour to show you, even more plainly, the causes that prevented the development of the country, in spite of your admirable constitution. The Magyars ever looked upon policy as the foundation of the State. Now a State can neither be based upon exclusive privileges, nor merely a liberal *form* of government. *Intellect* and *morality* are the only safe foundations of a State; where they are wanting, or if the people do not possess any inclination for the same, it is impossible for such a State to improve.

Where intellect and morality do not exist, the

State is without any internal support; for then every one commands, and does what pleases himself, but no one acknowledges the duty of obedience. The powerful hand of a guide will ever be missed, and confusion, destruction, and unpunished crime will be found but a poor substitute for order and justice. The people will be the prey of those above them, and the government officials employ absolute power, because the masses generally are utterly without capability of improvement.

I have shown, in my foregoing letters, that tolerance was to be found less among the Magyars than any other tribe living in Hungary; that when religious freedom issued from Germany,— the land of enlightened progress and intellectual emancipation, it was the Magyars who opposed it with the whole strength of their unjust power. It is now my intention to destroy an illusion of the Magyars, which has not the smallest fraction of truth for its foundation, but which they themselves always believed, and would fain compel England and Germany to do the same. It is not the wish to lessen the warlike renown of the Magyars, but simpy the love of historical truth, that obliges me to dispel this illusion. The Magyars have always represented themselves as the "bulwark of Christendom;" but my last letter has already proved that it was the Magyars who, under the pretext of religion, or love of freedom, allied themselves with the heathen, and invited them to enter the land, to protect them, and bestow honours upon them.

John Zapolya was the first political rebel that ignominiously betrayed his country by inviting the Turks to lay it waste. If Zapolya had had either faith, character, or the slightest spark of honour, he would, from religious, as well as national motives, have leagued himself with his lawful king to deliver Hungary from the inhuman oppression of the Turks: but ambition was too deeply seated in his heart, and, for the sake of the bare title of king, he sacrificed his country to the arch-enemy of Christendom.

The second rebel, Bocskay, had the same elevated notions of freedom and civilization as Zapolya; perjury, deceit and lying, were the weapons he employed against the court. The Austrians were everywhere calumniated; the government was accused of negligence when the nobles were allowed to do as they pleased, and if it acted upon its own authority it was accused of cruelty and oppression. When Bocskay was pressed hard by the Germans, he placed himself under the protection of the Turks. He, as Christian, preferred submitting to the Mahommedans sword in hand, to employing peaceable and constitutional measures in the service of his king and country. But murder and treachery were rife in his own camp. His own particular friend was the traitor Michael Kútay. One of his principal tools was the gipsy Blasius Lippay, captain of the Hajducks, who plundered and robbed whenever there was an opportunity, but his arrogance and immense wealth at last excited the displeasure of his rebel leader, at whose command he was murdered at a midnight revel. As soon as this disgraceful act was accomplished, Bocskay accused his murdered friend of having had a secret understanding with the Austrians.* What a fearful insight does this give us into the demoralized nature of these men, who pretended to be fighting for a purer faith and liberty! Sigismund Rákotczy was a worthy compeer of Bocskay, although the Emperor Rudolph, but a short time before, had bestowed considerable estates upon him, and raised him to the rank of Baron of the empire. But ingratitude and treachery never

* Fessler, "Geschichte der Ungern." Vol. VII., p. 562.

ultimately succeed; where moral motives do not animate a political party, it is impossible for it to prosper. Though modern philosophers may ascribe the moving powers in the development of mankind merely to the force of intellect, yet iu the organization of society this force must be regulated by morality. It is certain that pure intellect always acts in accordance with the laws of nature, which are never in opposition to that moral and spiritual harmony which flows through the universe.

The great historian, Fessler, in his account of Sigismund Rakotzy's treason, shows us the fearful consequences of the misconception of the simplest fundamental principles. He says, "Let no benefactor count on the gratitude of the reciever of his benefits, if he has attacked the most sacred rights of the liberty of conscience, either in reality or in the receiver's imagination. The worst man never *sincerely* sells the fundamental principle of his real or supposed worth, either for court favour or titles."* Fessler does not seem to remember that wickedness on the part of the benefactor cannot excuse ingratitude and treachery on the part of the receiver of a benefit, or that a

* Fessler, "Geschichte der Ungorn," Vol. VII. p. 583.

ANSWER IV.   97

man of honour can never receive a benefit from a bad man without bringing himself down to the level of his benefactor. The sentence, "The worst man never *sincerely* sells," contains a very doubtful morality. The man who has the slightest regard for honour *never* sells his principles; but if he once sullies his honour, either for the sake of ambition or avarice, he cannot purify it by treacherously deceiving the man who has bought him. But, unfortunately, policy, the science of exigencies, has often made a necessity of every meanness. Hungary gives only too plain a proof of the dreadful influence such degeneracy of all moral fundamental principles exercises upon the social development of a State. No one will be surprised that Bocskay, William Drugeth, his Commander-in-Chief, Michael Kátay, the Chancellor of the Empire, Francis Rakotzy, the Chief Councillor of State, and George Szécsy, as well as the greater number of princes and lords of Hungary, Transylvania, and Wallachia, decreed, "that the freedom of openly exercising their religion should be granted to the Roman Catholics, and the followers of the Augsburg and Swiss confession of faith, to the *exclusion of all other sects.*"

In this we see the narrow-minded tendencies of

these heroes of freedom. They were without the slightest regard for justice or liberty. Unitarians, Socinians, Arians, Jews, and Mennonites, might be persecuted; they only gave freedom to those whom they chose. It was impossible for them to appreciate the real value of the word tolerance; therefore, they had no right to complain of the intolerance of the opposite party. The time, however, must come when the progress of civilization will not allow the State to interfere with the religious opinions of individuals. The principles which the immortal Joseph II. acknowledged, and wished to bring into life,—in which noble purpose he was hindered by the uncivilised, narrow-minded Magyars,—will, in time, become the moving-spring in every State of the civilised world.*

After Bocskay had placed himself at the head of the rebellion, and, in the place of the blessed Virgin, who was always represented on the Hungarian

---

* That which Hegel says of Frederick the Great may, with greater truth, be said of Joseph II.: "He was not only a philosophical Emperor, but an altogether peculiar and unique phenomenon in modern times." Joseph II. took up religious principle in its secular aspect; he was by no means favourable to religious controversies and did not side with one party or the other, but he had the consciousness of Universality, "which is the profoundest depth to which Spirit can attain, and is Thought conscious of its own inherent power."

flag, inscribed the glorious sentence, "Isten velünk senki ellenünk," (If God is for us who can be against us), and introduced into his camp Luther's song, "Eine feste Burg ist unser Gott" (A castle of defence is our God), as a battle hymn, he sent Stephen Korlát and George Kekédy to escort the Mahommedan Kiaja to Constantinople, to implore the protection of the Turkish Court for his Christian league. At the same time, this rebel Christian sent the Sultan some *well-formed German boys*, who had fallen into his lawless clutches; they were dressed in purple, and adorned with mitres.* It could have been no *Christian intentions* which induced him to deliver up these unfortunate youths to the tender mercies of the Turks.

What a fearful contrast does this present to our view! On the one side, we see hypocritical humility, piety, and religious enthusiasm; and, on the other side, nothing but acts of the blackest and most crafty tyranny and barbarity! Yet you are surprised, and cannot think how an inexplicable, unfounded hatred against the Magyars has arisen. Surely you cannot suppose that the inhuman cruelty of sending German boys as an

* See Fessler, "Geschichte der Ungern," Vol. VII. pp. 565 and 566.

offering to the Turks was calculated to win the love and gratitude of the German population. If you had ever seriously studied the history of a country, you would be aware that the greatest effects frequently arise from the most trivial causes; but you seem inclined to believe that a continual scorn and mockery of all human rights can have no effect on the historical development of a race.

You are right when you say that the Austrian Government risked its independence by the Concordat, because Austria, by that act allied itself with an element which, till now, has everywhere opposed a free political development; but, if you wish to be consistent, you must also allow that freedom will not be promoted by an alliance on the part of the Magyars, either with the Turks, or any of the barbarous Slave nations living in European Turkey, or the tyrannical despot seated on the throne of France, or the Czar of all the Russias. Such an alliance would soon destroy the integrity and independence of Hungary. But a short time would elapse, and Hungary, torn in pieces by civil factions, would become the prey of Panslavism. I have no doubt that, if you had the choice given you between Panslavism and

Pangermanism, you would prefer the former. You think you would be better able to trifle with the Panslavists, and thus restore the times of Zapolya, Bocskay, Tököly, and Rakotzy. The only reason for Bocskay's allying himself with the Turks was, "to strike fear into the hearts of the royalists, and to make use of their interested cooperation, giving them no more advantages than circumstances would permit." But this doubledealing,—this open as well as secret perfidy,—could not possibly ensure the success of their enterprise, it could only have a demoralizing effect upon both people and country. Although Bocskay allowed himself to be made king of Hungary by his ally; yet he made peace with the Emperor-king, and was, at last, poisoned by his accomplice, Kátay, who, being accused of the murder, was thrown into prison.*

The nineteenth Article of the conditions of peace which the rebels sent to Vienna, to be laid before the Archduke Matthias, is a most remarkable one: "Offices of the State are only to be given to native Hungarians, without regard to their creed; and not only are no foreigners to be allowed to occupy these posts, but even the descendants of

* "Bethlen apud Katona," Chap. I. p. 661.

naturalized foreigners, in the third generation, are to be excluded.*

What a contrast is this to the protection which England affords to everyone living on British soil! If we wish to study the art of governing, we ought to take England and her wise constitution into consideration.

But now we must turn our attention to the rebellions under Gabriel Bethlen and George Rakotzy, which are distinguished by the same perfidy and want of stability. Rakotzy treated with the Swedes, and closed an alliance with the French through the ambassador, Antoine Croissy; but, at the same time, he received a command from his Turkish ally to make peace with Ferdinand. Rakotzy, however, without any consideration for his oppressed fatherland, or for the people, who were reduced to misery by war and rebellion, worked only for his own ambitious purposes, and led his allies, as well as the Emperor of Austria, according to his own capricious humour. In order to carry out his magnanimous plans, he made use of the meanest tricks of lying and hypocrisy. But he concluded peace at last; and the Turks were so enraged at the addition made

* Katona, Tom. XXVIII. pp. 436—451.

to his possessions, that they again threatened to overrun Hungary. Rakotzy at last died, and left to his country the prospect of still greater sorrows and sufferings. Notwithstanding all this, all the acts of the Empire and the Diet prove that Ferdinand himself endeavoured to subdue the differences of opposing parties, and that his patience and firmness with the refractory prelates was almost inexhaustible.

The facts that I have brought before your notice show, that it was not the Germans who allied themselves with the Turks, but the discontented Magyars, who were continually asking for their assistance, and supplying them with German prisoners. Instead of combining their forces to drive the heathen from Europe, whose religion and government prevented the slightest intellectual improvement, the proud Magyar Lords crawled in the dust at the feet of the Sultan, and tried to make use of the arch-enemy of their faith as a means of advancing their own private interests. I cannot understand how the idea, which you, as well as many other writers entertain, that Hungary and its lords have been the "bulwark of Christendom," has gained ground. As we proceed, we shall see that it was not the Magyars who drove the Turks out of Hungary, but German soldiers, German knights, German generals, and German dukes, who conquered the infidels with their strong arms and invincible bravery. And now the Magyars reward Germany with the bitterest hatred for having poured out its blood like water for the deliverance of Hungary, and bestowed it upon them as their inheritance. And once again the rebellious Magyar Tököly leagued himself with the heathen Pasha Ibrahim, and commenced a war of extirpation against the Germans, till Charles von Lothringen, Louis von Baden, Count Stahremberg, Joachim Rüdiger, Count Dünewald, Prince Braunschweig Lüneburg, Count von Scherffenberg, John Charles von Thürgau, Prince von Waldeck, etc., and their valiant German Landsknechts, cavalry and artillery, delivered Hungary from the traitor to king and country,—that disgrace to the name of a Magyar, that contemptible slave of the Turks,—Emmerich Tököly. Charles von Lothringen and Maximilian of Bavaria, by a successful stratagem, drove the Turks out of Buda, and thus the capital of Hungary fell into the hands of the lawful king, after it had been in the possession of the followers of Mahomed for 150 years.

ANSWER IV. 105

We must regret that King Leopold was induced, by the malicious and cowardly Italian, Caraffa, and his abandoned mistress, Elisa von Ujhely, to adopt too severe measures, and that the execution of these measures was left in the hands of this bloodthirsty monster; but even this may be excused when we consider the intolerant spirit of the times. The principal sufferers in Upper Hungary, the seat of Protestantism, were Germans; the names of those who were put to death by the Italians, Caraffa and Federigo Giuliani, Draheim of Dantzig, and the Swabian Burghard, prove the truth of this assertion. Sigismund Zimmerman, Kaspar Rauscher, Gabriel Ketzer, George Heischenker, George Schönleben, Simon Feldmeyer, as well as Slaves and Magyars, are mentioned among the number of the victims. Leopold, however, was at last informed of the cruelties of this fanatical disciple of Torquemada, who openly offered a reward of 600 florins to anyone who could discover a new instrument of torture, and kept thirty executioners constantly employed. As soon as the King heard of it, he instituted a commission of inquiry, abolished the Court of Blood, and deprived Caraffa of his office. The Jesuitical friends of this monster so misrepresented the real facts of the case that they induced the King to give him the order of the Golden Fleece.

We who endeavour to look deeper into this complicated chain of circumstances, cannot but think it impossible for Hungary to develop itself while it was the theatre of such horrible crimes. The Emperor-kings had constantly to contend with treachery, rebellion, and perjury. Whenever an opportunity offered, a Magyar partisan, under the pretence of protecting the constitution or religious liberty, would ally himself with the enemies of his legitimate king: whether that king was liberal or tyrannical, whether he gave them freedom or deprived them of what they already possessed, whether he was tolerant or intolerant, the Magyars did not care,—their sole aim was to rid the country of their rulers. The same bitter animosty exists between Austria and Hungary that existed between England and Scotland till Queen Anne united them under one Parliament; then, and not till then did the sanguinary struggles cease, England and Scotland, although different in the development of their social and religious relations, assist with their united material and moral capacities in making Great Britain powerful and prosperous. The Highlander joyfully sheds his blood in defence of the banner that bears the arms of England, in connection with those which belonged to Scotland when it was an independent kingdom. Scotland's thinkers, philosophers, geologists, physicians, authors and poets increase the glory of England's literature; and that Englishmen joyfully do homage to the talent which Scotland produces was plainly to be seen at the great Burns' festival. Englishmen never dreamed of getting up an opposition demonstration like the Magyars with their Kazinczy festival in Pesth in opposition to the Schiller commemoration. What mockery to compare a Schiller with a Kazinczy!

The wounds which civil war had inflicted on the country were hardly closed; no reorganisation had taken place since the hot breath of war had withered its vital powers; commerce and trade were almost dead, and even agriculture had hardly revived, when Francis Rakotzy again raised the standard of revolt. Two thousand men, principally robbers and impoverished Magyars* took the field. They carried twenty flags bearing the inscription which you so appropriately placed on

* See Fessler, "Geschichte der Ungern." Vol. IX. p. 501.

the title page of your pamphlet: "*Pro Deo, patriâ, et libertate!*"

Their patriotic intention was to destroy the little order that still remained with their scythes, pitchforks, cudgels, and flails. Rakotzy placed himself at their head after having entered into secret treaties with Lewis XIV and the Poles; and again eight years of civil war desolated the unhappy country. It was, however, at last put an end to by the peace of Szathmúr.

It is now my intention to quote a few passages from Rakotzy's Memoirs, which were written in French during his exile in Turkey; and they will show you that this man was magnanimous enough to confess openly what were then the real causes of the fall of Hungary. Although these extracts are short they will amply confirm my statements, and prove how erroneous is your superficial representation of the condition of Hungary; and if the Magyars are not too infatuated to listen to the voice of *truth*, they may serve as a lesson to them in the dark and threatening future which lies before them.

An ambitious despot was even then seated on the French throne, a despot whose whole aim was to bring the world under the dominion of the

French, and one who apparently as well as really entered into alliance with the enemies of Austria. This tyrant, whose government must be condemned, even when looked upon from the most indulgent point of view, as far as regards moral honour and general interest, was the most determined enemy of all religious freedom; his repeal of the Edict of Nantes obliged his Protestant subjects to leave their country; half a million of the most deserving and industrious Frenchmen were obliged to fly for safety to America, Germany, and England.* We must not allow ourselves to be dazzled by the brilliant literature that was developed during his reign; this literature was poisoned by false servile flattery, and had a most enervating influence upon the social morals of the people. Francis Rakotzy looked upon Louis XIV. just as you and your party look upon Louis Napoleon,—as "*the deliverer of Europe;*" he looked to him for the redress of wrongs which circumstances had normally developed, and which could only again be remedied by the normal development of circumstances.

Francis Rakotzy says in his prefatory epistle,

* See Blanqui, "Histoire de l'Economie Politique." Vol. II p. 10.

which is dedicated to the eternal *truth*, "The greatest part of the misfortunes about which I write has been caused by *ambition*, which we can never sufficiently repent. . . . . . The inordinate love of rule which existed in Hungary acknowledged no laws, and poisoned all grades of society. . . . . . The people refused to obey the magnates on account of the natural hatred which existed between them and the Hungarian nobility" ("à cause de la haine naturelle qu'il y a entre le peuple et la noblesse Hongroise ").

In writing about the discipline of his soldiers, Rakotzy says: "My soldiers had hardly been quartered in the town, when a wild noise of shouting, screaming, and shooting, was heard. The soldiers had not been able to resist temptation, but had seized all the wine which was to be found in the cellars. Their officers, who were of the same stamp, did not set them the example of sobriety; they were even worse than their inferiors."

About the nobility Rakotzy writes, "The nobility of the neighbouring countries were also favourable to me; and they sent some of the poorest of their order to observe the condition of my forces, and discover my intentions. . . . ."

ANSWER IV.   111

These few words entirely confirm my statement, that want of confidence in those who pretended to be working for the weal of Hungary, always lamed every enterprise. They had no trust in one another; not one of them believed that the other could have the general interests at heart. The advancement of their own private interests was their sole aim, and they betrayed one another directly these interests were injured, or even only threatened.

About the rebellious troops Rakotzy writes: "The number of robbers without the camp (for they were much more like robbers than soldiers) that laid waste the estates of the nobility, increased from day to day. By giving themselves out as my soldiers, they were able to oppress houses and castles that they could not otherwise have robbed and plundered." The outcasts of society, under the pretext of fighting for liberty and fatherland, always flock together, and, in the general confusion, are able to give themselves up to every vice. It is very certain that nothing but energy, firmness, and unanimity, on the part of the leaders of a political agitation, can rescue the country from anarchy.

As I have before said, when Rakotzy writes

about the King of Hungary, he takes the same peculiar views of that monarch's position, which you have adopted. In spite of the Magyar constitution, "*this model of self-government,*" as you are pleased to term it, he accuses the head of the State of having done nothing in Hungary. Should the Magyars be accused of having broken their oaths, Rakotzy says: "These oaths were extorted from the Hungarians contrary to all law or liberty, and were so outrageous that it would have been sinning against their descendants to have kept them." If such opinions did not even now prevail amongst those who aspire to rule the fate of Hungary, we should merely attribute them to a time when the Jesuits were all powerful, and the most perverted ideas of morality were rife among the upper classes. We cannot therefore be surprised that nothing durable was the result of a rebellion which was headed by men who openly avowed such principles. What king would have the power to oblige a self-governed nation to commit perjury?—and if it does commit such a crime, no one but the most perverted casuist would so lightly excuse it. We cannot be astonished at any abnormal opinions which may exist, when the citizens of a state do not pay the

ANSWER IV.   113

slightest deference to the Decalogue, but even excuse the man who, for political reasons, does not hesitate to break these commands, which are the only sure foundation of social unity. Rakotzy was as much imbued with this Jesuitical casuistry as you are; for he attributes all the social crimes of the Magyars, such as avarice, disorder, laziness, ignorance, and roughness of manners to Austria. Your model of self-government can either never have existed, or it had a very opposite effect to the self-government which existed in England, in the German free-towns, in Sweden and in Holland. With inimitable simplicity the great statesman Francis Rakotzy adds, "All that I have mentioned is nothing but the bitter fruits of the paternal government of the House of Austria, under whose rule the nation has contracted the habits of a spoiled child, which is not the fault of the nation, but of its father." But as soon as this father (like Joseph II.) tried to lead the spoiled child towards social improvement, the child stamped and screamed and resisted the heartless cruelty of that monstrous parent, and undertook to govern itself; and the inevitable results of this self-government were dissension, anarchy, civil war, and submission to foreign rule.

Rakotzy asks: "When have we ever had an Austrian king who erected colleges for the improvement of youth? When have we ever had a sovereign who established academies for the cultivation of the arts and sciences? What monarch has ever employed the nation either at court or in war? Who ever introduced commerce and trade which would have guarded it against the evil consequences of idleness?"

In none but a despotic monarchy is the king obliged to undertake such duties, which of right belong only to the citizens. In constitutional monarchies the sovereign is jealously excluded from all interference in such matters. Has a king of England ever improved the commerce and manufactures of the country? No; it was the *people alone* who did it. If the Queen of England or her government would venture to interfere in these affairs, a rebellion would be the consequence; but Francis Rakotzy in childish ignorance laments this non-interference on the part of the government. How then can you compare the Magyar constitution with that of England?

Rakotzy was of opinion that the court was the place where the nation would be weaned from all profligate habits! *Risum teneatis!* When and where was the court the place where the nation was weaned from all profligate habits? The cloven foot is but too plain in this phrase. Offended pride speaks in the person of the Magyar statesmen. He saw others shining at court, and it would have gladdened his heart to see the nobleman of his own country rioting at the Austrian court. As we have already mentioned, as long as the court did not interfere with the exclusive privileges of these oligarchs, everything went on smoothly; but, directly it attempted to abolish their exclusive rights, for the sake of the further development of the State, according to the more modern theories of State-policy, these oligarchs took up arms. I think even you must confess that it was a most difficult task to strike out the right path between constitutionalism and despotism, to both of which they laid equal claims.

I will give another extract from Rakotzy's Memoirs, concerning Bocskay, which will be a fresh proof of how Hungarians were compelled to raise the standard of revolt in *defence of freedom*: "As Bocskay had been educated among Germans, he was very favourably disposed towards them; consequently, many of the real liberals did not trust in him. They consulted, therefore, as to how they might disgust Bocskay with the Germans. They determined to write a letter in his name, but without his knowledge, which would make him appear suspicious in the eyes of the Austrian General Batta, and they sent the treacherous epistle by a stranger to him. The *stratagem* succeeded. The General was greatly incensed, and determined to proceed against Bocskay The conspirators discovered his plans, and, at the same time, informed Bocskay that the General not only considered him suspicious, but intended to arrest him on a certain day."

What knavery! Denunciations, calumnies, perjury, and forgery were the weapons with which these liberals fought for the most elevated aspirations of humanity! Such an act is called a *stratagem*, when according to general ideas of justice, it ought to have been punished with imprisonment. Why did the *friends* of Bocskay enter into such a conspiracy which, if it had not succeeded, would have brought their friend to the gallows? Because they imagined that policy excused that and all similar actions. But I repeat that truth and honour must be the moving principles in politics as in private life. When machinations, lying, and calumnies, form the impure basis of any political act, the progress of civilization is only checked, never promoted. If we require honour and liberality of a government, we must set them the example. A nation will never conquer the enemies of freedom with lying and denunciations!

In writing about the peasants, Rakotzy says: "They could call nothing their own but their *soul!* in consequence of which, they entertained such bitter hatred against their lords, that they thought of nothing but vengeance."

Again, in writing about the Magnates, he says: "In their hearts they generally preferred the Austrians; for they were not willing to expose their property and estates to the chances of a revolt, partly because the family and person of Count Berzsenyi (Rakotzy's confidential friend) was not held in great consideration, and they did not care to side with me because they feared to be placed in an inferior position to the Count."

Great and important advantages were always sacrificed to small and individual interests!

Rakotzy's opinion of the nobility was the following: "The nobility lived in retirement on their estates; they were thoroughly indolent and gave themselves up to drunkenness. They occupied themselves more with bringing children into the world than educating them. Many nobles brought up their children either to commerce, which was beneath *(sic!)* them, or to the mechanical arts; and they considered themselves extremely fortunate if they could make advocates and solicitors of those who possessed the most talent, and these numerous lawyers were the cause of almost all the Magyar lawsuits." *

In the character which Rakotzy gives of his most faithful friend, Count Berzsenyi, we shall see a portrait of all better educated Magyars: though refinement has somewhat weakened the old faithfulness, they have, in olden, as in recent times, imitated the French opposition tactics,—burning down every bridge between themselves and the adversary, and holding everyone for a traitor or a spy who was not of their opinion. This has destroyed all mutual confidence, and has rendered the unity of powers even still more difficult than in olden times.

Berzsenyi remained true to Rakotzy through all the dangers of a civil war that lasted for eight years; he followed him into exile, and was faith-

* Compare this passage with the description I gave in my second letter of the social condition of Hungary.

ful unto death. We will now read Rakotzy's description of him: "Berzsenyi suffered no rival in power.* He was unbearably harsh towards his inferiors. When not on duty, he was implacably biting and satirical; careless when in earnest, bitter and contemptuous when angry; an obstinate admirer of his own opinions, he held those of others in low esteem; eloquent in conversation, hesitating in action; incapable of deciding in doubtful matters he always cast the disagreeable burdens on other people's shoulders.

"*Berzsenyi was incapable of making any difference between the talent and ability of men.*

"It was almost impossible to reconcile the Magnates to him. Although they were apparently willing to give him precedence, on account of his rank and the esteem in which I held him, yet none of them were his sincere friends. *One often came to me, to accuse and calumniate his friends,* after he had discussed both me and my actions pretty freely with the self-same friends."

* This one sentence of Rakotzy's is an exact description of all the heroes of 1848. Everyone wished to usurp the power for himself; they tolerated no competitor in office. Everybody wished to do everything by himself in the administration of the country. This mania for rule drove everyone to govern, and no one to obey; because, till 1848, the privilege of being a politician was a prerogative of birth and nationality,—not of merit, extensive knowledge, or intellectual superiority.

It is an historical fact that the manner in which war was waged under Rakotzy was distinguished by greater consequence and heroism than that of 1848—49, and the peace between Austria and Hungary was more generally favourable to the Magyars; but the general results of both movements were the same, because the primary causes, the elements of the struggle, the moral, social, and political means towards the end were the same. Similar causes must produce similar effects. Scorn and mock the Germans as you will, the historical fact remains, that thinkers and theorists, empirical and idealistic philosophers, always precede every great political change in the life of a nation. Bacon first enlightened the world with his ideas before Cromwell could destroy the despotism of the age. Intellect destroys prejudice; intellect cultivates and organizes States; intellect converts wildernesses into habitable places; intellect subdues the rude powers of nature, tames the power of fire, makes air and steam serviceable to man, roams through seas, measures the world, and fathoms the most secret laws of prolific nature. Intellect continues to progress, in spite of the tyranny of superstition or politics. But the old Magyar constitution gave these privileges, which they denied to intellect, to birth, caste, and descent; thus they only dreamt of giving liberty to the press, or of wanting to make use of that liberty,* after having governed Hun-

* I will here just give the reader an idea how far our lawgivers, in 1848, in the first blush of their enthusiasm for liberty, endeavoured to give the people the key-stone of freedom,—that keystone which the English lawyer, Bracton, in his work, "De Legibus et Consuetudinibus Angliæ," between 1262 and 1268, declared to be *liberty of the Press*. As the Hungarian magnates, prelates, and nobles of the kingdom, never troubled themselves much about literature, they forgot to give or to use the liberty of the Press. And this is the principal reason why we have no thinkers, no historians, and no philosophers; why we have no literature, and are enchained by the modern social and political French ideas; why only an ephemeral newspaper literature existed in Hungary, without anyone taking the trouble to devote himself to more earnest and important studies. The newspapers were chiefly in the hands of impoverished advocates, who, in default of lawsuits, turned to literature as a last resource; and from those men the government demanded £1000 (10,000*fl.*), security (the Austrian government required only £200). Besides this, it was ordained that for every violation of the Press laws, an author should be punished by from 2 to 6 years' imprisonment. By this high security it was intended to make the Press accessible only to the wealthy magnates; and the liability of incurring such a long imprisonment entirely prevented all freedom on the part of authors. But § 11 was the most curious part of this law: the punishment for offending a *common citizen* was not the same as that reserved for offending a *government official*. If the latter were attacked, the fines and imprisonment were much more severe than in a similar offence against a non-official. And this was what they, in utter perversion of all ideas of justice, called *freedom of the Press* and equality before the law. While in England the private character of every citizen is sacred, and anyone committing a libel, even in a letter, is indicted for felony, in our country the law endeavoured to protect the government official from the attacks of the Press, but gave up the private character of every citizen for a less heavy fine, to the attacks of the same. The real state of the case was this: the men of the opposition were bent upon becoming government officials, and therefore they wished to silence in advance the voice of public censure.

gary for eight hundred years. The old Hungarian constitution was like the fig-tree in the parable, which was hewn down and cast into the fire, because it bore no fruit, nor gave any promise of it in the future; and no modern statesman will mourn its loss.

The only thing that remains to be done with Hungary is to plant a new tree,—but the soil in which it is planted must be judiciously chosen. If a just and equal division of the burdens of the State, inviolability of the head of the government, obedience to the laws, equality of every citizen in the sight of justice, and perfect security of the person and property, should be the soil chosen for the new tree, then Hungary, even as a member of the Austrian empire, will be free, prosperous and powerful! . . .

ANSWER V.

Notwithstanding the time which I have devoted to the study of the modern history of Hungary, I find it difficult to give an opinion upon the present condition of that country. If I wished to make my task as easy as you have done, and draw my information from the gossip of the Parisian Imperial Journals, I fear I should not advance the cause of truth. I will however confine myself to a few undeniable facts, and prove to you that although Hungary at times has been politically oppressed, yet in its social relations it has made immense progress since the abolition of the constitution which you so much lament.

For ten years the aristocracy of Hungary has been humbled! But it has been a wholesome humiliation. It was necessary for them to learn that exclusive privileges, without any other advantages, which can afford effectual support in time of need, are without value. If they sincerely wished for the progressive development of the country, they must have turned their attention from political gossip to the management of its material interests. If they have learned wisdom by experience, general progress must be the consequence; agriculture must have improved, roads have been made, means of communication opened, and markets for the sale of raw produce discovered.

The equal taxation of magnates, nobles, burghers and peasants, has created a feeling of equality in Hungary, which before was only found in the mottos at the head of a few radical journals.* The discovery of gunpowder in its time had a most beneficial influence upon the progress of mankind. The rude physical powers were made subservient to the might of intellect. The different orders of society were suddenly placed upon equal footing. Lords and vassals, knights and squires ceased to exist. The gloomy fortified castles lost their terror. Agriculture, commerce, and manufacture were protected against the robbing, riotous, brawling nobility. Modern society in its present formation is greatly indebted to this

* In 1848, notwithstanding all the endeavours of the press, it did not succeed in abolishing that injustice which obliged only the peasants and the Jews to pay bridge-toll in Pesth, while the magnates, prelates, nobles and citizens, could drive, ride, or walk over the bridge without paying.

invention.* The discovery of gunpowder had less effect upon Hungary, because the use of firearms was reserved exclusively for the nobles. At the *battues* the peasants were employed in beating up the game, but they were never allowed to use guns. Besides this, firearms were so expensive that the peasants were not able to buy them. While standing armies were formed in England, Germany and France, the Hungarian peasants were sent out of the country to fight in the ranks of the Imperial army, and the nobility, according to the feudalism that prevailed in the country, was the only military power,—a cause to which we must ascribe that rude domineering spirit which was antagonistic to all peaceable employments.

* Hegel says, on the effect of the invention of gunpowder, in his Lectures on the Philosophy of History, Bohn's edition, p. 419: "We may indeed be led to lament the decay or the depreciation of personal valour. The bravest, the noblest, may be shot down by a cowardly wretch at a safe distance in an obscure lurking place; but on the other hand, gunpowder has made a rational considerate bravery—intellectual valour—the essential to martial success." The immortal Herder writes about the discovery of gunpowder as follows: "It is incredible how much, in the modern condition of Europe, is to be ascribed to this invention, which has subdued the spirit of feudalism more than all the councils of the Romish Church, promoted the power of all governments more than all popular assemblies; prevented the blind massacre of personally embittered armies, and limited the warfare which it produced. See "Ideen zur Philosophie der Geschichte der Menschheit." Vol. II. p. 514. Buckle also treats of the effects of the discovery of gunpowder in a very excellent and original manner. See "History of the Civilization in England." Vol. I., p. 185-190.

Equal taxation must have, however, changed and transformed the opinions of the nobility. Equal taxation must have effected in Hungary, that which the discovery of gunpowder was incapable of doing. It must be looked upon as a powerful means towards overcoming the invincible pride, the mocking contempt of everything in the shape of principle, and the moral degeneracy of the nobility. That you speak against taxes *in general*, more particularly against the high taxes imposed upon the nobility, does not surprise me, nor will it surprise anyone else who has become acquainted with the organization of the Magyar State through these letters. It is really time to give up the utterly false ideas of taxation in those States that wish to keep pace with other countries.

Franklin says: "In all parts of the world men must die and pay taxes;" but the noble Franklin either did not remember, or he was ignorant of the fact, that a human caste, the Hungarian nobility, were to be exempt from this necessity; or perhaps we ought to say that Franklin could not imagine such a case in a half-organized State.

Adam Smith has embodied in four general

maxims the fundamental principles of taxation.*

I. "The subjects of every State ought to contribute to the support of the government."

Every exception of this rule leads to that ruinous inequality in the social condition of a State which must prevent development and progress.

II. "The tax which each individual is bound to pay, ought to be certain, and not arbitrary."

You say the Austrian officials have violated this principle; if so, they ought to be punished, for they must be responsible to the government as well as the people for a just account of the taxes. But even in countries like England, where the justice of equal taxation has long been acknowledged, we hear continual complaints of the rudeness and violent barbarity of the tax-gatherers. You are mistaken if you imagine you have told the world a startling novelty, when you complain of the coarse roughness of the tax-collectors. As a Magyar, you may be surprised at the idea of all citizens taking an equal share in the burdens of the State; but as a politician you ought to welcome that idea as the dawning of a better future for Hungary.

* "Wealth of Nations." Book V., ch. ii.

III. "Every tax ought to be levied at the time or in the manner in which it is most likely to be convenient for the contributor to pay it."

You complain that in Hungary tobacco is a monopoly, and that a most oppressive tax upon the smoking public is the consequence; but I will reply to this complaint in the words of Adam Smith: "Taxes upon such consumable goods as are articles of luxury are all finally paid by the consumer, and generally in a manner that is very convenient to him. He pays them little by little, as he has occasion to buy the goods. As he is at liberty, too, to buy or not to buy, as he pleases, it must be his own fault if he ever suffers any considerable inconvenience from such taxes."

IV. "Every tax ought to be so contrived as both to take out and to keep out of the pockets of the people as little as possible over and above what it brings into the public treasury of the State."

Every mistake which the government makes in taxation the government alone must expiate. The mistakes that it is possible to make, Adam Smith reduces to the following four points:—

"First, the levying of the tax may require a great number of officers, whose salaries may eat up the greater part of the produce of the tax, and whose perquisites may impose another additional tax upon the people."

In time, such an error must necessarily lead to a sanguinary revolution. It is extraordinary that in the old world, i. e., before the introduction of national credit, revolutions were always connected with the bankruptcies and money embarrassments of private individuals, just as, in the modern world, they are the consequences of State bankruptcies and finance embarrassments. The Hungarian revolution of 1848, and the last French revolution, are, however, exceptions to this rule. The man who placed himself at the head of the former, was continually troubled with pecuniary embarrassments, and the leader of the last French revolution was a desperate man, who only saved himself from the debtors' prison by a *coup d'état.**

"Secondly it may divert a portion of the labour and capital of the community from a more to a less productive employment."

"Thirdly, by the forfeitures and other penalties

---

* A word which cannot be translated, as the fact which it designates is contrary to English principle. Such are also the words, *esprit* (instead of "common sense") *fricolité, galanterie, petit maitre, coquette, étourderie, point d'honneur, bon ton, bureau d'esprit, lettre de cachet,* etc., words which denote the peculiar disposition of the French nation, and convey notions unknown to every other people.

which those unfortunate individuals incur who attempt unsuccessfully to evade the tax, it may frequently ruin them, and thereby put an end to the benefit which the community might have derived from the employment of their capitals."

"Fourthly, by subjecting the people to the frequent visits and the odious *examination of* the tax-gatherers, it may expose them to much unnecessary trouble, vexation, and oppression."

That every government, be it Austrian or Magyar, will have to encounter many obstacles, in the levying of taxes, is the natural consequence of the former organization of the State. Equality of taxation will long remain a difficulty. Austria cannot have succeeded already in rooting out the current idea, "Why are we princes, counts, barons, prelates, or nobles, if we have to pay taxes like the plebeians?" which is deeply seated in the hearts of the Magyars. As soon as a despotic government begins to make no difference between persons and classes, it takes up a revolutionary position against an antiquated system, because the equality of every citizen in the sight of the law is one of the fundamental ideas of modern State-policy. This is the position of Austria, with regard to the Magyar constitution. You can surely remember the cry of horror which issued from the nobles, both rich and poor, when Széchényi's exclamation of "Adózunk" ("Let us pay taxes!") resounded through Hungary.* Even in 1848 little was said about equal taxation. There were a few just men who acknowledged the necessity of the nobles, as well as the commoners, paying taxes according to their possessions, but that does not cancel the fact that, during the revolution no one thought of taxing the nobility.

The Austrian government has secured landed property to the peasants, for which it has indemnified the nobility; but taxed it, at the same time, according to their landed property, which is divided into various classes with regard to its fertility. A learned Theban remarks, in the "Westminster Review," "That the nobles have managed, with the help of the compensation paid to them by the Austrian government, to get through the last twelve years, but they will not be able to continue to pay such immense taxes much longer."† Certainly not if the nobility, *more patrum*, do nothing. It is almost incredible that an English political critic should bring this as an accusation

* See Széchényi, "Adó es két Garas." Buda: 1844.
† See "Westminster Review," New Series, No. XXXIV., p. 475.

against the Austrian government; but, though a man may be quite capable of giving an opinion about the general condition of his own country and literature, as soon as he ventures to pass sentence upon foreign nations, their organization, literature, and social institutions, he is guilty of the most absurd paradoxes and hypotheses. Such a man has not the link of connection of cause and effect, and without knowing this, he wanders in a maze, without a chance of finding Ariadne's thread to lead him to the regions of light and truth. There are some people who are even worse than this, for they judge foreign nations from hearsay. Our learned friend in the "Westminster Review" may really know an Hungarian who pays £50,000 (?) taxes; but he forgets to tell us what is the amount of his income. Even though a Prince Eszterházy, or a Count Bathyányi, may have to pay £50,000 (?) taxes, they have plenty left to live upon. High taxes are only a proof of a country's wealth. If taxes were levied which were beyond the power of the subject to pay, this would only show us the unreasonable tyranny on the part of a government; but neither you nor the Reviewer have troubled yourselves to prove that this has been the case in Hungary. There is no country which is taxed higher than England, and yet England is a *free* country. A man who pays £70 per annum for a house in the City pays about £20 yearly in taxes. Such a man, however, is no rich prince, with landed estates, large sheep farms, dairies, castles, forests, etc., but simply a cigar or colour-merchant! What Englishman would think of calling the government a despotic one because that man has to pay taxes.

The Hungarian magnate, compelled by the high taxes, will cultivate his land to the best advantage, and think of means and ways to increase his capital. He will cut down trees, breed sheep, and trade with wool; while the cigar tradesman, besides the high taxes for his house, has to pay 3*s.* 4*d.* per lb. for tobacco, and 9*s.* 6*d.* per lb. for cigars duty to the government; yet he must live, and support and educate his family. And yet no one ascribes the necessity of imposing high taxes to tyranny on the part of the English government, because it is a well-established fact that a State cannot exist without taxes. That, however, which is clearly necessary, is often looked upon by short-sighted statesmen as a crime, especially if it can be made use of in opposing a government which is hated. " Equality of taxation, therefore, as a maxim of politics, means equality of sacrifice*." If every individual were penetrated with the duty of personal sacrifice for the general welfare, he would give support and power to the State. When once the nobility see this necessity, and understand the use that is made of taxation, the greatness of the productive powers of a country like Hungary will soon appear.

Those who possess can easily give of their superfluity, if they only know how that superfluity is to be employed. It ought to be employed in paying the army, in keeping up the administration of justice, and in promoting public instruction.

But now we must take into consideration an almost unconquerable difficulty which Austria has to overcome in Hungary. The army is jealously watched: for the different nations of Austria have not yet learned the all-important lesson of interesting themselves for a "great whole." The army is as much divided in itself as all the other institutions. The Hungarians would be willing to pay for a national army; but for the Austrian imperial forces they have no inclination to contribute taxes. But if they were to look upon it from a proper

---

* See "Principles of Political Economy," by John Stuart Mill, Vol. II. p. 370.

point of view, they would prefer belonging to a great and powerful whole, than to an insignificant part. If every canton of Switzerland were a separate State, without any centralized supreme power to manage the finances and army of the whole, we should see one canton becoming the prey either of two or three united cantons, or some *disinterested* neighbour. This was the case with the smaller States of Italy in the Middle Ages; this is even now the case with Germany, whose immense intellectual, commercial, and industrial powers are paralyzed by division; and this will be the case with Austria, if it sacrifices the idea of a powerful and united State to the idea of separate nationalities. Instead of having a strong and mighty empire in the East, we would see a number of small republics lifting their impotent heads; and these republics, impelled by national hatred, would mutually destroy each other, because, in that corner of Europe, there still exists so much material belonging to the Middle Ages, that cannot reconcile itself to the modern principles of government, but looks upon warlike deeds as the mission of humanity.

Austria has greatly improved the administration of justice. There is now *no distinction of persons*, either before the civil or criminal courts of law. Trial by jury has not yet been established, but the first great step towards it,—the equality of every citizen in the sight of the law,—has already been taken, and this is of great importance in the development of a State.

To give the reader a superficial idea of the administration of justice in civil matters before 1848, I will mention, amongst the many legal remedies known as Admonitio, Protestatio, Inhibitio, Depositio Causæ, Revocatio Procuratoris, Prohibitio simplex et cum onere, Appellatio, Oppositio, Reoccupatio, Repulsio, Novum Judicium, etc., only one as an illustration of the means by which a law-suit could be dragged through three or four generations:—Caius goes to law about an estate that is worth 100,000 florins, which Titus has illegally possessed for twenty-five years. During this space of time, Caius has been collecting the proofs and documents necessary to establish his claim; during these twenty-five years he has been paying the lawyers, and informing the judges with the nature of his case. At last sentence is pronounced; the estate is declared to belong legally to Caius. The sentence is sent to Titus, and Caius demands its immediate execution. The defendant, Titus, however, laughs at the plaintiff and the verdict, and has recourse to "Oppositio;" *i. e.*, he opposes the legal execution of the sentence of the law, remains in possession of the estate, and lives upon its income, in accordance with the law, for he begins an oppositional law-suit. The conclusion of one law-suit is but the commencement of another. The lawyers of Titus, by their intrigues, manage to drag the case on for ten years longer, at the end of which time Caius is again triumphant. What becomes of Titus? He has to pay a fine of 200 florins (£20), and Caius loses the ten years' income of his estate, about 40,000 florins (£4000), without the slightest compensation.*

This kind of justice has ceased, the government having introduced a more equitable mode of proceeding, since 1848. Whoever is only slightly acquainted with the simplicity and justice of the Austrian civil and criminal code, cannot be sufficiently thankful that the "Tripartitum," with all its voluminous nonsense, ambiguity, and want of decision and intelligence, has given way to more just ideas of right and wrong. The administration of justice, as well as the whole of our policy, was subject only to mere outbursts of passion. Love

* See Fessler, "Geschichte der Ungern." Vol. X. p. 257.

and hatred, sympathy and antipathy, had more to do with the government of Hungary than the immutable laws of justice, truth, and virtue. A conservative was looked upon by the opposition as "a villanous traitor." Not only his political opinions, but his private character, were violently attacked; he was exposed to open insult when in society, —which is even now the case with the Austrian officials. This conduct must necessarily exasperate the officials, and they misrepresent every speech that has the slightest reference to the government, and denounce every assembly as a conspiracy, merely because they themselves are looked upon as outcasts of society. Neither the imperial nor the liberal party are sufficiently advanced to understand that every individual has a perfect right to express his independent opinions, by which means Conservatives as well as Liberals give their opinions a chance of victory, because they would be obliged to trouble themselves to give reasons for these opinions. The time when privileges could be demanded at the sword's point belongs to the past. Whoever sows hatred, envy, and suspicion, can never hope for a harvest of love. By an implacable enmity in political matters no State can make progress; for such a contest would end only with the extirpation of one or the other party. Not by physical strength, but by intellectual energy and moral principles alone, can one party assume and maintain its superiority over another.

Kant says that truth alone can be developed by allowing the antagonistic propensities of mankind full play. The experiences of the past must teach us useful lessons for the future. The destruction of one class of society, the exhaustion of our powers by never-ending hostilities between the different nationalities, a mutual oppression of adverse political or religious parties, neither of them allowing free expression, will never convert our unhappy country into a well-organized State. The charge of intolerant oppression, which the Radicals bring against the more moderate politicians might be brought, with even more truth, against the Radicals themselves. Tolerance in politics is even more necessary than in religion. Love for the static element of any religion has generally degenerated into intolerance and thus prevented the development of mankind; but this aberration can be more easily excused than political intolerance, as it is always supposed to be based on moral principles. Above everything it is necessary that each individual should look upon himself as a member of the State. The general welfare can only be promoted by a free and equal discussion of every opinion. Individual freedom must be given to everyone living on Austrian, as well as Hungarian, soil. This personal freedom is endangered if the Magyars are permitted to press their own language upon the other nationalities. This experiment has been tried once already, and they are now again about to try it. They complain that the Austrian government wants to Germanize the country. This complaint may be well grounded; but how much more just is the complaint when it is brought against a nation without literature, scientific resources, great thinkers, or historians! While in Hungary there is not a man, even if he is only slightly educated, who cannot speak German, yet there are whole regions where the Magyar language cannot procure even a drop of water for the thirsty wanderer. Notwithstanding, the Magyars, in 1848, seized the church-registers, which were written in the language of the different nationalities, and burnt them, because they were not drawn up in Magyar; moreover, they maltreated and hung those peasants, as traitors to the country, who dared to resist this barbarism. They did not endeavour to assert their supremacy by social means, in the field of science or improvement, but they asserted it *jure fortioris*, with the help of the law; and they tried to impose the language of a minority upon a majority. You yourself have numbered the population of Hungary as follows:—

Magyars	6,150,000
Germans	1,589,715
Slaves	4,626,965
Wallacs	2,374,472
Jews	350,000

Vends, Bulgarians, Italians, Frenchmen, Armenians, Clementines (?), Greeks, Montenegrins, Gypsies, and Bohemians, make the sum total to be 15,500,000 inhabitants. By introducing now the Magyar language six millions would compel nine millions to adopt a language which does not furnish the means of acquiring any knowledge of the progress in medicine, mathematics, geology, cosmology, philosophy, statistics, history, mineralogy, chemistry, etc.,—a language which could not even assist them in trading with any one of the neighbouring countries, which, in fact, would isolate them from the whole European world. And now let us compare this with the supposed injustice of the Austrian government, which has undertaken, by a propagandism of German culture and science, to oppose the daily increasing Panslavism.

Are you and the Magyars so short-sighted as not to understand that, in isolating yourselves from the Germans and Germany, you must necessarily become the prey of that encroaching Panslavism, which will not even offer you the delights of a refined and tasteful literature for the loss of all your liberties and your language. Hitherto the officials only have been required to speak German; the different races are allowed to speak their own tongues. Authors can write in what language they please; the learned man is permitted to serve his own especial nationality by enriching it with standard works. There are not more obstacles in the way of Magyar than German journals; on the contrary, the Magyar journals are permitted to reason much more freely. The German newspapers would soon receive a warning from the police, if they presumed to follow their example. The tyrannical oppression of which you complain is felt much more by the Germans than the Magyars. Instead of wasting their powers in trivial jealousies, the Magyars would do well to make themselves acquainted with their true position.

Although numerically superior, the Flemmings in Belgium will never obtain the political supremacy over French, Germans, and Walloons; French and Italians will never gain a superiority over the Germans in Switzerland; and the Magyars can only then become really powerful if they exchange the idea of national supremacy with that of sound liberty,—if they will exclude all dialectical discussions, in future, from their political program.

It is vitally necessary for Hungary to enter into commercial relations in the north, south, east, and west, and these relations would require an extensive knowledge of different languages. The Magyars, like the Russians, have a peculiar talent for languages. Instead of losing by cultivating them, they would only gain. In all *German* schools, the students are compelled to learn French and English; German and French are taught in every English school, and the Swedes are obliged to learn German, English, and French. No Magyar, however, thinks of complaining that the English wish to "Anglicise," or the French to "Gallicise," the world. Close commercial relations, thirst for knowledge, and desire to become acquainted with the thinkers of these great nations, induce the people to study carefully the means by which great thoughts are expressed. These means, however, are only valuable when they are capable of expressing ideas. If a language is void of ideas,—if great thinkers have never made use of it in expressing their thoughts, —the value of the language must necessarily fall to the ground. Your complaint, therefore, of being obliged to learn German, is one of those childish outbreaks of national pride that arises, not from careful and quiet consideration, but from political antipathy, which, in Hungary, always made even the administration of justice subservient to the passions of ill-regulated men, suffocated every feeling of right, and hindered, in every direction, the development of the Hungarian State.

The ruling authority of a State like Austria requires a universal language to express its will: this language, historically as well as practically, can be none other than the German. The commerce, manufactures, and science of Austria are entirely German. The educated people of all nationalities speak German; and, although the Germans are physically, *i.e.*, in quantity, inferior, yet, intellectually, *i.e.*, in quality, they are infinitely superior to all the other national fragments.

While German papers, like the *Vienna Press*,* have from 30,000 to 40,000 subscribers, Kossuth's *Hirlapja*, in the height of the Hungarian Revolution, could only boast of 8000 subscribers, though the Conservative German paper, *Pesther Zeitung*, had 6000, and the Liberal German paper, *Der Ungar*, 6500 subscribers. The latter had in Budapesth alone, 2500 subscribers, while Kossuth's *Hirlapja* could not circulate more than 1800 copies in the capital.† The Magyars could develop themselves in a literary and social manner, if, instead of complaining, they would sit down and study, think, and write; but the Magyars will have much to do either to surpass, or even to raise themselves to the level of the Germans.

Lord John Russell is quite right when he says, in one of his speeches : " In a short space of time, seventy to eighty millions will speak the English

---

* I purposely avoid mentioning an official Gazette, and allude only to a party paper.

† These facts are taken from notes made at a general meeting of all the editors in Pesth, over which the minister Klauzál was invited to preside, in order to discuss the possibility of substituting a simple wrapper for the envelopes in which the newspapers were generally despatched. The suggestion was, however, rejected, because the majority of those present agreed that they could not rely on the post-office employés, who would be sure to take advantage of the opportunity offered to circulate the papers amongst their own acquaintances, for a trifling profit, instead of delivering them to the proper subscribers.

language: may we not therefore hope that these kindred nations, speaking the English language, each deriving its *pedigree of liberty* from a common ancestry, each inheriting the English Bible, each reading Shakespeare and Milton, each divided into many denominations of Christians, but each allowing complete liberty of worship, will unite in the glorious task of peaceful conquest and bloodless victory?"

This peaceful conquest, this bloodless victory, is the aim of civilizing Germanism, which is represented in the east by Austria; this aim will, however, never prevent a free development of the different languages of the various nationalities. Even the Emperor Joseph II. only made German the official language; he never forbade the Magyars to speak their own tongue, which, in his times, was only spoken in the lowest classes of society; and it was merely the spirit of antagonism which induced the Maygars to revive their almost forgotten language. There is no doubt that this spirit of opposition is necessary to the development of the human race,—that it alone makes the continual intellectual friction possible, and alone feeds the flame of intellectual progress. Kant calls this spirit antagonism; Buckle, scepticism—the Germans prefer calling it criticism. It is the spirit of discussion, the spirit of opposition, that is, the spririt of criticism, which compels a nation to progress. Criticism should everywhere be greeted as the dawning of truth. Criticism knocks first at the gates of the *ancien regime* in knowledge as well as in the government of nations. It was criticism that put to flight the fabulous forms of the Titans, that robbed the winged dragon of its terrors, that converted astrology into astronomy, that created out of the diabolical art of the alchemist the wonderful system of chemistry. Criticism crushed the iron building of superstition and prejudice,—pronounced it a crime either to drown witches or burn heretics.

This criticism has always occupied a very difficult position; the analysing power of the intellect, even up to the 18th century, was looked upon as the most terrible and formidable of powers,—it has almost been dangerous to know more than people generally. Criticism fought out a path for itself through the wildest thickets of philosophy and politics. In the highest offices of government, people are beginning to perceive that the development of mankind cannot stand still, and that this development of mankind can only take place when the various political parties of a State make no pretensions to exclusive infallibility,—when individuals as well as masses are of opinion that, when a man has arrived at maturity, and is conscious of the power of his understanding, he has a perfect right to make use of that power as he pleases. Criticism in science, as in the art of governing, is the forerunner of experience; and experience often induces us to adopt very different opinions to those which hereditary prejudice taught us, and which have often become a kind of second nature to us. We must, however, have the power and courage to combat everything that is contrary to the laws of nature, so that we may be able to place society upon a firmer and more just basis than that of the continually changing, merely *relative* historical privileges, which, when based upon the development of any language, becomes still more uncertain and fluctuating. Where are the four Hellenic races—the Doric, Attic, Ionic, and Eolic? They were obliged to unite their forces before they could secure the grandeur of the Peloponnesus. What became of the English Heptarchy? Egbert laid the foundation of England's greatness, by uniting that which was divided. What would have become of the Umbrians, Oscians, Latins, Etruscans,

Sabellines, etc.? It was only as a great and powerful whole that the Roman Empire arrived at an elevation which compelled the then known world to lie prostrate at her feet. What would have been the fate of the various tribes in France,* the Normans, Celts, Basques, Iberians, Goths, Gauls, etc.? Would France ever have been able to play her arrogant game in the history of the world, if the small duchies of Normandy, Lorraine, Burgundy, etc., which were always at war,

---

* Weber, on the Popular Elements of France, quotes the following passage from Ranke: "The principal tribe of the whole country was the Romanized population. Their language, traditions, and peculiar institutions, were closely related to the Italians and the Spaniards, then groaning under a foreign yoke. Besides this tribe, we find remains of the Celts, as Bretons, which were continually reinforced by immigrants from the coasts of Great Britain, who delighted in scorning law and subordination; of the Iberians as Basques, who showed but a doubtful submission, interrupted by frequent and violent hostilities, whilst the German immigrants were faithfully attached to the Establishment of Church and State. Their origin was, for a long time, apparent. The Goths renewed even their race and name on the frontiers of Spain. The Franks and the Romans were most closely united on the banks of the Seine, in the heart of the country, where the Merovingian kings took up their residence, and formed round Paris the powerful dukedom of Francia; but gradually the Latin Franks separated themselves from the Germans, with whom they were closely allied in manners, mode of thinking, and the principles of their institutions. At last, the Normans overflowed the country, and brought the French coasts into communication with the North of Europe. The overpopulation of the European West, *i.e.* the *Roman* world, which still occupied a considerable part of it, and the Germanic tribes, which assumed to themselves the universal dominion over land and sea, met on this soil, within these limits."—See Weber's "Allgemeine Weltgeschichte." Vol. I. pp. 539, 540.

had not been united? No: that which had been isolated and powerless, was only then able to drive nationalities divided amongst themselves victoriously before it when it was transformed into a great national whole. Where are the traces of the Chaukes, Angles, Franks, Cheruskians, Usipetes, Katts, Shamavans, Sigambrians; where the Allemans; where the Goths, and their allies the Herulians, Rugians, Vandals, Gepides; where the Visigoths and Ostrogoths? During the degradation of Rome, Germany was the nurse of national primitive force, youthful freedom, social intercourse, and elevated morals. The great Roman Empire has disappeared; it was based upon national exclusiveness. Germany is now about to be united, and enjoy the fruits of that primitive national power in glorious freedom; but Germany's present and future is based upon intellect and knowledge. The sword has only brought misery upon her, as well as upon every other country. The spirit of German culture, German civilization, German tolerance, assists the continual development of mankind.

The great work of amalgamating the different small nationalities, none of which are capable of governing the other, belongs to Austria. Do you really believe that the Magyars are sufficiently powerful to transform the hostile nationalities into one harmonious whole? The numerical majority of the Slaves must in time obtain the physical superiority over the Magyars. Who would have the right to forbid the Slaves to make their own language the language of the State? And, if the Slaves once obtain the superiority, who can prevent the Czar of all the Russias from enjoying the fruits of that superiority? Nothing limits the principle of Russian despotism so much as the critical and philosophical Germanism, with its perfect imprint of spiritual and individual freedom, which even England's thinkers envy, and the development of which is the whole secret of German supremacy in the field of thought.

It is a well-known fact that the Hungarians look with such utter hatred at everything that comes from Germany, that they would prefer oppression under any other government to the most liberal German administration. But who would take the place of this other government? Is it to consist of Magyars, who would only think of carrying out their dividing, isolating tendencies? What would the Croats, Servians, Germans, South Tyrolese, Upper and Lower Austrians, and

Styrians, say to such a government? Do you think that they would suddenly give up all sympathy for the great and intellectual Germanism, and quietly resign themselves to the subordinate position of Magyar vassals? No; for though Magyars and Croats have lately been upon a more friendly footing, yet there exists such bitter hatred between these two tribes, that the present friendship would soon be put to flight by disputes, quarrels, and sanguinary civil strife. It is only because the German element exercises a subduing, guiding, and humanizing influence over both these tribes, that they unite in hatred of the intellectual superiority; but as soon as they again are freed of the civilizing chains of Germanism, they will remember the hostility that, in bygone days, existed between them, and endeavour to wash out the reminiscences of the past in each others heart's blood. This is also the case with the Slovacs. As a proof we may bring forward the latest religious movements amongst Lutherans and Calvinists in Hungary. Whilst the Magyar communities refused, 120 Slovac communities accepted the concessions granted by the Emperor of Austria to the Protestant Church. To brand these as traitors to their country, would be too severe.

If the minority would be handled thus, what could the Magyars expect with reference to their own minority, when brought into relation with the overwhelming majority of the other nationalities?

These facts will give the reader an idea of the difficulties that must be overcome before Hungary can be reorganized; and, at the same time, he must perceive that an independent Magyar State with Magyar supremacy is impossible. The Austrian Empire must become *a whole*, based upon German right, knowledge, and policy, allowing each nationality perfect freedom to develop its own language. It is, however, totally impossible to make the nationality of any of the different tribes in that part of Europe the political foundation of the existence of an Eastern Empire. If the Magyars really cared for freedom, they would avoid all exclusive national demonstrations; but the trivial hatred of *dialectical* dissension is carried so far that you even, as statesman, complain of the beggarly contribution which the Austrian court pays to the German theatre in Pesth, while the great Magyar nation has to support the Magyar national theatre. Do you consider it the duty of the Austrian court to assist the latter as well as the former? What a request! It certainly requires a peculiarly perverted mind not to be ashamed of making such a complaint on behalf of a nation which would like to be considered as the future lords of the East. And this nation, which had to concentrate all its national efforts upon arts and literature, and, according to your own confession, was allowed full freedom in it, looks with envious eyes upon the assistance which the Court of Austria affords to a troop of German actors! Where such opinions and motives are mixed up with politics, nothing truly great can be the result; but let all nationalities in Austria stand calmly on the same ground of right and liberty; let us no longer strive for *dominion over one another*, but let *everyone* be free!

Besides the political steps which Austria has taken, and which I intend to discuss in my last letter, it has done so much for the improvement of commerce and trade that it has even alarmed constitutional Bavaria. Guilds and trade-corporations have been placed upon such liberal footing that a Radical writer, in the *Deutsches Museum*,* openly confesses that Bavaria, notwithstanding its constitution, which has existed for half a century, has

* This is one of the best weekly papers; it is published by Robert Prutz, and edited by Dr. Brockhaus; Leipsig, 1860.

not reached the point already attained by despotic Austria, viz. to introduce a trade-regulation that frightened the honest Bavarian burghers out of their wits. The organization of trade-corporations in Austria, was till lately chained down by the most ridiculous prejudices of the darkest Middle Ages. The number of masters in all trades was limited: if a vacancy occurred, it was filled up only by such as had previously obtained the right of settlement. Though the established trade might produce bad work, a new comer did not stand any better chance of being admitted into the guild because he was a clever artizan; on the contrary, every effort was made to keep him out of the corporation, because he would stand in the way of those who remained true to old customs. The potter was not allowed to clean an iron oven, the poulterer accused if he sold sausages, the bookbinder impeached if he employed a needle instead of paste in making portfolios. The opinion prevailed that the paying public existed only to support the artizans, and that it was not the duty of the artizans to satisfy the buying public with their work; and this utterly false idea prevails, even now, throughout Germany, amongst the government officials,—they look upon the public as their servant, and will not acknowledge that they are the servants of the public. If the people and the officials were only sufficiently advanced in their political development to acknowledge the truth of this assertion, the officials would fulfil their duties conscientiously, and the people would no longer consider the officials as their paid enemies, but look up to them as useful servants of the State as a whole, who deserve esteem, payment, and gratitude, for their laborious work, and particularly to obtain support from the people by a free and unlimited exchange of ideas. Unnatural causes must necessarily produce unnatural effects. The mistaken idea of the position of officials and people has created an hereditary hatred on both sides, instead of which each party ought to try and advance each other's interests, for the sake of the general welfare.

The guild-regulation had not only a prejudicial effect upon the development of trade,* but also upon morals, of which I could mention innumer-

---

* This tyranny was carried to such an extent in Hungary, with regard to the Jews, that they, as artisans, were not allowed even to open a shop. Jews were never allowed to become masters of a trade, and yet they were always represented as a people averse to labour, and addicted to hawking. The Jew was not allowed to acquire property, he was not allowed to carry on any trade; yet they accused him of being idle, and merely fit for traffic.

able examples, but I will content myself with one, for which I have the authority of the *Deutsches Museum*: There was a young, and in every other respect, an honest workman, who was employed in the workshop of a widow. He loved her daughter, but he was unable to obtain for himself the license to pursue the business, though the widow was willing to resign it in his favour. At last, in despair, he married the mother, to obtain the right of practising his trade independently, although he afterwards lived with the daughter!

This is, unfortunately, but the natural consequence of such a dreadful organization,—the result that might be expected from such an abnormal regulation. By the abolition of these trade-corporations, Austria has done much for the cause of general improvement.

Neither ancient privileges, yellow parchments, nor international treaties can lead either individuals or nations to that civilized and moral freedom which ought to be the aim of every government. It is only a right perception of the laws of morals and nature, and perfect individual freedom, which will enable a nation to obtain this end; but the caste-creating constitution of the Magyars never had such a noble aim in view.

If Hungary wishes to constitute a future State, it must surely have profited by the administration of the last ten years. Roads have been mended, railways laid down, banks and boards of trade established, wages raised, the export and import augmented; and all these facts must have materially assisted in developing the powers of the country, if a miserable self-murdering spirit had not induced the landed proprietors to remain inactive. Intercourse with all parts of the Austrian Empire has been greatly facilitated by an imperial patent issued in the year 1857, in which the necessity of procuring passports for travelling in the interior of the Austrian Empire was abolished, so that people were enabled to travel wherever they pleased within the Austrian dominions. Therefore your assertion, "that it is impossible to go even to the next village, to see a sick friend, without a passport," is entirely without foundation. These hyperbolical accusations are not calculated to promote a healthy political condition, after the feverish social convulsion that has shaken Hungary to its foundation.

The future of the Austrian Empire must be based upon true *freedom*. It must be based upon reasonable freedom; a freedom which pays no regard to difference of belief or language,—a freedom which shall hold the right of possession and personal liberty as sacred as the right of thinking, speaking, and writing freely. Each individual must be allowed to devote his capabilities to the State; no one must be excluded, either on account of his nationality or his creed. There must be no respect of persons before the law; the same justice must be delivered to government employés, soldiers,* and peasants, by judges who cannot arbitrarily be deprived of their office. These are the elements upon which Austria's future must be founded, and then everyone living upon Austrian soil will acknowledge with pride that he is a citizen of a State whose government secures him the highest and holiest blessings.

No State can exist without a government which has not only to watch over the spirit of the laws, but over their inviolability. Such a government

---

* Soldiers must be subject to a court-martial for breach of discipline; but for any violation of the civil law they must be subject to civil courts of justice. By this means only will the soldier cease to form an exclusive caste; the citizen will no longer look upon him as his paid enemy, but as his brother, and the defender of his home and of the honour of his country. The soldier will no longer cease to be a citizen; consequently he will not treat the citizen as his inferior. The civil code of laws will deter the soldier from placing himself upon an equality with the common thief, and a more elevated spirit will influence the whole military administration.

has great duties and responsibilities, which it is only able to fulfil with the vigorous assistance of every individual citizen. Nothing should be more respected in a State than good-will towards that State. If religion is to be held in higher, holier estimation, it must acknowledge no principle at variance with the normal development of the State, or that might hinder its general progress. The wisest path for Austria to pursue would be to separate Church and State; for it is often the case that, where Church and State are closely united, hypocrisy and bigotry are the consequence, more especially when the Church is in possession of immense tithes. Concessions are made for the sake of worldly advantages, which, for the sake of truth and progress, ought never to have been thought of. True, religion has the same end in view as a well-organized State; because religion and State ought to advance the happiness and freedom of mankind.

Plato, in his Republic makes disposition the principle of his State, and, consequently, he ascribes everything to education. This is exactly opposed to the principles of modern Statesmanship, which wishes to make everything dependent upon *individual will*. But where can we find the certain assurance of the welfare of the united whole in this individual will? This individual will must learn, first of all to respect the laws. It is only respect for the existing and inexorable laws which, in the first instance, may have been but the efflux of despotism, that will insure the life and progress of a State; and this life and progress must never be poisoned by mutual *suspicion*.

Wherever suspicion, as it was and is now the case in Hungary, divides society into two parts, without regard to principles, but according to blind national prejudice, murder, desolation, and misery, are the consequences of any revolution. A State which is founded merely upon national or moral sympathies or antipathies, becomes the prey of tyranny and slavery, which is infinitely worse than the oppression of a single despot. Dispassionate and thoughtful intellect can alone be considered a fit guide for a State. Virtue alone may lead even to murder. This was only too clearly the case in France. Hegel says that "Robespierre set up the principle of Virtue as supreme. . . . .

Virtue and *Terror* were the order of the day; for subjective virtue, whose sway is based on feeling, only brings with it the most fearful tyranny. It exercises its power without legal formalities, and the punishment it inflicts is equally simple,—*death.*"*

Much worse, however, is the condition of that State which relies neither upon virtue, honour, religion, nor freedom, but merely upon the insupportable tyranny of accidental difference of language.†

---

* See Hegel's "Lectures on the Philosophy of History," p. 470.

† Gibbon in the "History of the Decline and Fall of the Roman Empire," says that "public virtue, which among the ancients was denominated patriotism, is derived from a strong sense of our own interest in the preservation and prosperity of the free government of which we are members." This public virtue can never reach a high degree in a country like Hungary, in consequence of the many different nationalities, none of them being sufficiently cultivated to obtain a mental superiority over the other, none of them being numerous enough to form a decided majority, if political rights should be granted, not as hitherto, to one, but to all nationalities without distinction. Should this not be the case, the less favoured fragments of nations would fall into the position of vassals and merely tolerated strangers with reference to the privileged one. When the Romans saw themselves compelled to employ foreign mercenaries in their legions, the feeling of unconquerable patriotism deserted the troops of the great Empire. Hirelings (and foreign nationalities, even when settled in a country which affords them no political rights, must always be considered as hirelings!) stepped in the place of invincible patriots, and Rome sank deeper and deeper, till it at last fell. Honour and religion supplanted patriotism; then came the *free* German tribes, and the mighty Roman Empire broke down under the heavy blows of their clubs. The Magyar patriotism, with all its enthusiasm, has never effected anything of lasting greatness. In overvaluing their real powers, the Magyars relied on the old Roman, or modern French, political theories, both of which are based on exclusive patriotism, which develops a spirit of protection, restricts progress, and makes freedom impossible.

ANSWER VI.

It is with sincere sorrow that I perceive, from the tone of your letters, that you belong to that adventurous party that has fixed its hopes for the future on Louis Napoleon. At the commencement of your first Letter, you exclaim, with pathetic sentimentality, to your countrymen in the following remarkable terms: "That Louis Napoleon, among the princes of Europe is the only heir of the Russian Autocrat, Nicolas, and stands at the head of France strongly concentrated (?). But here there is a difference to be made, which is that Napoleon III. has, at the same time, raised the flag of 1848, on which were inscribed the sacred words, *independence* and *nationality*. Immortal glory to him if he continues (*sic !*) faithful to that flag!" This one passage is sufficient to condemn you and your party in the eyes of all thinking men in Europe; a party which is not ashamed of allying itself with the national despotism of the French, in order that it may gratify its own national vanity by obtaining, for a short time, the power of exercising a like despotism in its own country. Yet once again you are guilty of having perverted historical facts:—Who ever heard of "independence and nationality" being inscribed on any of the revolutionary banners of 1848? "Liberty, Equality, Fraternity," were the magic words that resounded from the banks of the Seine, inspiring thousands of honest hearts with an enthusiastic love of liberty, driving them into misery and exile. It was only when the Socialists of Paris disgraced this device by the sanguinary insurrection of June,—when the proclaimers of these principles ignored them, and set out to subdue Rome,—when, unmindful of them, they elected the namesake of a soldiering freebooter, and allowed him to overthrow the hardly-established constitution which he had sworn with a sacred oath to defend,—it was then only that Europe became aware how absurd and contradictory were the grand words that had thrilled through every heart. And you do not blush to say, in the face of modern history, that Louis Napoleon has raised the banner of 1848, on which were inscribed the sacred words, "Independence and nationality." The man of the *coup d'état*, who slaughtered thousands of unarmed citi-

zens on the Boulevards, who banished thousands
to the poisonous marshes of Cayenne, there to
contemplate the liberal theories of the "Idées
Napoléoniennes," who has established in France
an enervating, demoralizing policy; is it likely
that such a man should inscribe such words on
his banner, that such a man should acquire immortal glory, and that on such conditions he
should become all-powerful in Europe? In the
name of common sense, honour, and liberty, I
protest solemnly against this supposition.

The patriots who look to Louis Napoleon the
Décembriseur, for protection, are worthy of the freedom and independence which that despot is inclined
to bestow. But this declaration of yours must
open the eyes of England, as well as Germany, to
the principles which animate the so-called national
patriots, for which we feel greatly indebted to
you. Europe must perceive that the adventurous plans of Louis XIV. have been revived by
Louis Napoleon, who, inflamed by ambition and a
depraved despotism, tries to disturb the peace and
normal development of the world. Though Louis
Napoleon may not, like Louis XIV., contemplate
the possibility of placing the German imperial
crown either upon his own head or that of his

heir, still we see him looking everywhere for support for his yet unestablished dynasty. It is his wish that Italy should be powerful, but only under his protection; that Hungary should be independent, but under his protection; that a Rhine Confederation should exist, but only with his permission. If Egypt is not exactly colonized by Frenchmen, still it is drawn within the magic circle of French intrigues. He is about to make common cause with the Russians, and divide Turkey, out of pure enthusiasm for the independence of Europe.

When the siege of Vienna was raised, the letters found in Kara Mustapha's camp brought to light the secret understanding which existed between Louis XIV. and the Turks. It would not be difficult to discover an ample correspondence going on between Louis Napoleon, "the saviour of European society," and all those who, as stockjobbers, conspire against the safety of property; as Ultra-radicals, against the security of the person; as disturbers of the public peace, "*quand même*" against the lawful development of Europe.

All parties in Hungary, with incredible blindness, play into the hands of Louis Napoleon and

the Czar, and considerably advance the cause of
"Slavo-Gallic" universal despotism, for which
Louis Napoleon is as anxious as his illustrious
uncle, though he endeavours to acquire it in a
different way, by taking part in the farce of delivering oppressed nationalities. A clever gambler,
like the Emperor of the French, always keeps
several cards in his hand, so that, in case one fails,
he can play another. If the Czar and the halfeducated nationalities leave him in the lurch, he
can still fall back upon the Spaniards and Italians.
The idea of restoring the Occidental Empire has not
yet entirely disappeared, and if it should succeed,
Paris, of course, must be the capital. Should
France succeed in establishing a great industrial
confederation, by means of commercial treaties
strengthened by religious ties, those States which
the nephew of the great adventurer now patronizes
would see the necessity either of placing their
crowns upon his head, or of falling into the humiliating position of French dependencies: this is
almost the case even now. The Emperor of the
French imagines he has secured the support of
Victor Emmanuel, by allowing him to increase
his territory. Spain has brighter prospects: the
Queen, who has a daughter, is to be made happy

by the hand of the young Prince Imperial, and such a fortunate combination of circumstances would far surpass even Louis Philippe's Spanish marriages. By these means the Latin and Celtic races would be again united into one great Occidental Empire,* and the dark, casuistic despotism of a French Emperor would be able to oppose successfully the natural ideas of self-government, freedom, and progressive development which are the distinguishing characteristics of the Anglo-Germanic element, and thus not only maintain the old idea of the protective spirit, but extend it still further by amalgamating those tribes on the Lower Danube who, blinded by national pride, and reminiscences of a brilliant past, are willing to give a helping hand to the grasping ambition of Napoleon III. That this must be the natural policy of the French Emperor, is only the consequence of the traditions which have always been the foundation of the Franco-Latin political system. The Bourbons occupied themselves with the same intrigues; the Orleanists were unsuccessful in the same game; and Napoleon must pursue the

* See, on these and similar plans, Arthur de Grandeffe's "L'Empire d'Occident reconstitué ou l'Equilibre Européen assuré par l'Union des Races Latines." Paris, 1857, 8vo.

same scheme to enable him to retain his seat upon the throne of France, and ensure to his heir the possibility of reigning in the Tuileries, even if it were only for twenty-four hours.

True patriots can have as little hope that Louis Napoleon, the accomplished representative of restless and mischievous French policy, who suppresses every free word, perverts every political principle, and endeavours to limit thought and plant the spirit of protection even into the nervous and intellectual system of his subjects,—that this same usurper will assist Hungary in obtaining freedom, as the Hungarian Protestants under Rakotzy could expect that Louis XIV, who imprisoned, sent to the galleys, and executed amidst exquisite tortures, countless numbers of their fellow-believers, merely for the sake of their belief, could afford them protection against their oppressors.. Louis Napoleon will only do as he did in the last Italian war, that is to say, he will compel the Radicals to assist in advancing his own plans.

The Magyars ought by this time to have learned wisdom by experience; and by looking deeper into the hollow policy of France, they ought to perceive that it is not France that will save

Europe, because the principles on which the government of France is based, are like the principles which governed Rome, and they were not able to stand the test of time. From the end of the last century, up to the present time, France has played but a shifting part in the historical development of Europe. In philosophy, society, and politics; in fashion, superficial thought, and the destruction of civil order; upon the stage, in the saloon, from the pulpit to the public-house and the workman's associations, everyone on the Continent imitated the French.

The *diplomatists* copied the French in dancing, lying, and deceiving.

The *citizens*, with clumsy awkwardness, tried to adopt French manners.

Literary men in general, more particularly the Magyars, endeavoured to educate themselves in the French scepticism, as if doubt alone could advance civilization.

Even our *women* were seized with a mania for everything French.

The *police* was thoroughly penetrated with French ideas: to follow in the footsteps of a Fouché or a Vidoc, was the proud aim of many an aspiring police official. Through the whole of the Continent, every institution, every means by which mind and body could be subjected to the system of an unlimited protection, was transmitted to us by Frenchmen.

France, which has assumed the unlimited sway over the whole Continent, has been again chosen by the Magyars as the Mecca of their future freedom, and they look upon Louis Napoleon as their only prophet and guide in political matters. It may be as well to make the reader acquainted with the capricious humours, the moral worth, and the political power and grandeur, of that country over which Louis Napoleon rules, an irresponsible despot. As it may occur to this despot to play, with the help of our imbecility, again a prominent part in the history of the world, we must look closer into his character and that of the nation he oppresses. But, as I do not wish to be misunderstood, I must point out under what aspect, according to modern theories, I should wish the reader to consider the historical development of the French. I intend following out the same principles which guided me in my description of the Magyar State.

Man, as an individual forming so-called nations, is as much subject to outward influences as to inward impressions. The climate, food, soil, and the general aspect of nature, have an influence upon individuals, and consequently upon whole nations. The physical powers of an individual depend entirely upon the climate and food. The food, which is the production of the soil, has a most decided effect upon the constitution of the body, which again has untold influence upon the character and morality of the man.* As climate, food, and soil necessarily influence the life of a nation, the way and manner of collecting wealth is also greatly dependent upon them. Without wealth, knowledge cannot exist, and no nation can improve without knowledge, and without improvement it is impossible for a nation to obtain either religious or political liberty. What part of Asia could boast of the greatest civilization? That where the soil was the richest. What part of Africa? The same answer must again be given. What part of Europe has arrived at the greatest pitch of civilization? The central part, where

* It is a well-known statistical fact, that, while the population of France, for the last twenty years, has been continually decreasing, the population of England, in spite of the overwhelming emigration, from which France is entirely free, has since the beginning of this century, increased threefold. Still more striking is the degeneration of the French race; for the government has been obliged to reduce the standard military height to five feet.

the climate favours the possibility of the greatest activity, of the most extended industry, and of the greatest collection of wealth. But who advances the prosperity of the country?—who helps to increase its capital?—who makes the accumulation of interest and compound interest possible? The industrial classes. The citizen and peasant effect in Europe what the rich soil alone of Asia and Africa is incapable of effecting. But in France, till 1789, and in Hungary till 1848, these industrial classes were looked upon as a saleable property just like the soil; and the consequences of this led to the reign of the guillotine in France, and, in Hungary, to the fall of the ancient constitution. When I look upon mankind and nations in this light, if I suppose that Frenchmen, Germans, and Magyars, are not less influenced by impressions of nature than by their manner of thinking, reasoning, and their organization, my judgment must necessarily be devoid of party animosity, and depend upon the discovery of certain causes. Every thinker must be aware that it would be absurd to hate the effect, without endeavouring to remove the cause. On the contrary, we must learn how to avoid certain causes, to struggle against them, or to abolish them entirely, in order that we may escape their sure and certain effects.

France, like its soil and its climate, its wine and its women, has something most charming and attractive about it. Life is easier, consequently the manner of reasoning but superficial. Love is more inconstant; passion, though violent, more transient. The sun burns brighter and warmer, and snow rarely visits the southern part of France; therefore, a mental and physical indolence, and laxity of morals, are the distinguishing characteristics of the French people. Sparkling wines, cheap food, and an easily-excited imagination, are the principal elements of despotism and superstition, which always flourish where, by these means, the protective spirit is nourished.

Contrary to the Belgians, Swedes, Danes, Dutch, and Englishmen, the protective spirit, which was deeply rooted in the climate, and character of the people, and their Romish traditions, has developed itself in France. The chivalrous spirit of adventure inspired the Frenchman with a love for noble deeds abroad, bearing with him refinement of taste; but at home he oppressed the peasants, and scorned the tradesmen, deigning only to notice them if their wives or daughters were unfortunately handsome enough to attract his humiliating admiration. The Frenchman, with incredible blindness, sacrificed all power, privileges, revenues, and offices, to a frivolous aristocracy and a still more narrow-minded priesthood; he allowed those two classes to drain him of his all, and rob him of his rights. Even love,—at least, the possession of the loved one,—was an exclusive privilege of the aristocracy. If a nobleman, a count, or a duke, cast amorous glances upon the daughter or wife of a plebeian, the plebeian husband or lover was compelled to give way to the aristocratic admirer; or an action was brought against him, and the government interfered, assigning the wife to the husband or the lover, according to its *bon plaisir*. This assertion may horrify the reader, but I only state an historical truth. A hundred years ago, Maurice of Saxony fell in love with a French actress named Chantilly; but the young and talented *artiste* preferred the spirited author, poet, and musician, Favart, and married him. The great Maurice, who had never been looked upon with indifference by a *Frenchwoman*, was so highly enraged at the impertinence of the little commoner, that he petitioned the government to shield him from such disgrace. In conseqence of this complaint, Favart was arrested and thrown into prison. His miserable wife, to save her husband, submitted to the Duke; thus, for the sake of remaining the *virtuous* wife of Favart, she became the mistress of the great Maurice. When Favart was set free, he again, to preserve his freedom, was obliged to be conveniently blind to the whole of the horrible transaction.*

What a dreadfully confused idea of morality! Virtue is turned into crime, and crime is represented as a deed of heroism. The noblest feelings of a woman were sacrificed by government interference. The government itself was a monster, feeding on the blood of innocence, thus making every progress impossible, because it robbed those, whom it ought to have protected, of every better moral feeling. Under such circumstances, it is not at all astonishing that the French people learned only to destroy, but never to build up. Church and State, which mutually supported each other, restricted in every direction the spiritual development of the masses.

The State was the obedient child of a religion

* See Buckle's "History of Civilization in England," Vol. I. pp. 682 and 683.

that enchained the mind and tried to kill the body. What power was left for the unfortunate commoner? With regard to the nobility an exception was made in favour of the body. They were allowed to empty the cup of dissipation to the dregs. The mind and body of the nobility were undermined by gluttony and licentiousness, the two strongest instruments of despotism.

Till the death of Louis XV., the government of France was entirely in the hands of the nobility, and what was the condition of France? Can you discover no analogy between this land and Hungary, always excepting the great thinkers, artists, and poets, which belong only to France? In France the people formerly were nerveless, without power and courage, without mind; and for this reason, all the sanguinary revolutions resulted in nothing. It is not so easy to bring about a successful revolution. If a nation does not know what it wants, or if its wants are not in harmony with the eternal laws of morality, without which a State cannot exist, a revolution is useless; it can never succeed, because, with nations as with individuals, power is only the possession of those who are at unity with themselves.

Without any opportunity of learning to know their own wants, without leaders who could agree in one plan for the benefit of the whole, who thought only of gratifying their own prejudices and vanity, the French people were as incapable of forming a just idea of civil freedom as the Magyars.

Many years before the outbreak of the Revolution of 1789, the liberal thinkers of France, in consequence of the German Reformation and English Revolution, felt that they must also prepare for political reform. Every one who possessed intellect and talent began to study ardently the English language, English manners, and the English political institutions. Buffon, Montesquieu, Brissot, Helvetius, Lafayette, Mirabeau, Rousseau, Voltaire, Roland, and his celebrated wife, Segur, and Camille Désmoulins, all studied the English language, and endeavoured to make themselves acquainted with the English current of ideas. Even Marat wandered about Scotland for a long time, and made himself thoroughly master of the English, in which language he wrote two books: one of them, entitled "The chains of Slavery," was afterwards translated into French. Mirabeau himself confessed that he owed his great oratorical powers to his study of the English language, and a thorough knowledge of the English constitution.*

The French Revolution broke out after the two English Revolutions had secured to the English people those blessings without which freedom itself is not grateful, viz., perfect security to the person, and entire liberty to write and speak as they pleased. But what are the results of the sanguinary struggles which have taken place during the last seventy years in France? A contemptible despot, who till now has ignominiously betrayed all who put their trust in him, is seated on the throne. An infallible and indivisible church,—an all-powerful hierarchy, which is interested in keeping the people enveloped in the darkness of superstition, prevents every sort of lasting improvement. An ever-present police, that hears with a thousand ears, and spies with a thousand eyes, pays the reporter of every word unfavourable to the government more liberally than any man who performs a good action. A rude soldiery, which oppresses the people, wanton mistresses, vanity, orders of knighthood, festivals, intrigues, masquerades, *virtuous* "lorettes" upon

* See Buckle's "History of Civilization in England," Vol. I. pp. 657 and 665.

the boards, in the operas, in the ballets; here and there a *bon mot*, a "Charivari" without satire, except when private individuals are attacked, continual disturbances of the public peace, political prisoners in Mazas and in Cayenne, a gagged press, dissatisfied artizans, grumbling citizens, miserable exiles, and everywhere much ado about nothing! Even iron is taxed very heavily, not to protect the iron trade, because any English schoolboy of ten years of age is better acquainted with political economy than to give ear to such nonsense; but in order to prevent the speedy development of the State. Cheap iron makes cheap machines, and with cheap machines work is done quicker and better, and thus leaves the peasant time for reflection and education, which create a taste for freedom, exciting a love of order, out of which grows respect for the laws, by which the dominion of immorality is annihilated.

And what have the French gained, in spite of all their brilliant authors, in a social, political, and philosophical point of view? Nothing but contradictory results. And why these results of the struggles for freedom made by the French, as well as the Magyars? To point out, clearly and distinctly, the causes of these similar results will not only, at this present moment, be highly interesting, but of great use to anyone who is not indifferent to the development of the human race.

England was victorious, and became free, because the political movements in England were popular, and the aristocracy soon perceived that they could only acquire power, influence, and dignity, by supporting the people; consequently, a *bureaucracy*, which had the power of oppressing alike nobles and people, rich and poor, could not exist. If we go through the principal personalities of the English Revolution, we shall see that the political condition of England, and its modern liberal constitution, which is capable of introducing every improvement, is the work of the *middle*, or working class,—for I am not inclined to make much difference between the employer and the employed, which is, in reality but the difference between the contractor who pays, and the contracting party who works. Workmen cannot exist without employers, any more than employers without workmen; but where the employer is a clever, educated man, the workman will be sure to have a comfortable position. In the present condition of affairs everything depends upon the liberty which is given to the workman to raise himself to the position of a master. The most revolutionary men in England were, Cromwell, a brewer, Colonel Jones, a footman, Admiral Deane, the servant of a merchant, Colonel Coffe, the apprentice to a drysalter, Major-General Whalley, the apprentice to a draper, and Skipton, a private soldier. Of the two Lieutenants of the Tower, one was Berkstead, a pedlar, the other was Tichborne, a linen-draper; he afterwards became a colonel and member of the Committee of State. Colonels Harvey, Rowe, and Venn, were silk-mercers. Round that remarkable council-board were gathered Bond, the draper, Cowley, the brewer, Barners, the private servant, Cornelius Holland, the link-boy, Packe, the woollen-draper, Pury, the weaver, Pemble the tailor, Barebone, the currier. Besides these men, we may also mention, Colonel Harton, the footman, Colonel Berry, the woodmonger, Colonel Cooper, the haberdasher, Major Rolfe, the shoemaker, Colonel Fox, the tinker, and Colonel Hewson, the cobbler.*

This proves to us that the freedom of England was established by men, who did not understand how to turn fine-sounding phrases, but who had

* See Buckle's "History of Civilization in England," Vol. I. pp. 602, 603, 604.

grown up in the school of life, under the pressure of hard work, who had learnt to see that the privileged classes prevented the development of their powers, who, trusting to their honest rights, raised themselves to be masters of the country, and were contented with having obtained personal freedom for themselves and their fellow-citizens. This was also the case in Germany during the great religious Reformation. The son of a poor miner broke asunder the spiritual fetters forged by Rome, and procured us freedom, at least in matters of faith; and it is to be hoped that, after two centuries of religious liberty, Germany will obtain her political emancipation. Intellect has already prepared the way for ideas of freedom and union, which must be energetically carried out, and this will only be possible when those men who are accustomed to work step fearlessly forward, and lay the foundation of a new State on industry. Industry, to be successful, requires freedom; industry requires a free Press, and the right of assembling together, to carry out plans that an individual is incapable of effecting; industry requires law and order, but it must have the simplest kind of law, founded upon the most natural morality, which is expressed in the old sentence: "Quod tibi vis non fieri, alii ne feceris," "Do unto others as you would that men should do unto you." With this motto, it will not be difficult to oppose successfully pride of birth, tyranny, and all the old ideas of political economy which existed, and still exist, in France and Hungary.

France, up to the present time, has not been able to effect this, and will not be able to do it with those ideas of liberty, government, and morality now existing. It must first learn to reason from the Germans, and the application of principles in politics from England. England preceded France, not only in her great Revolutions, but also in a wise regulation of all social questions; and her philosophers were among the first to prepare theoretically the way for the practical application of political maxims. Bacon, the philosopher, lived before Descartes; Hooker, the moralist, before Pascal; Shakespeare, the poet, before Corneille; Massinger the dramatist before Racine; Ben Jonson, the satirist, before Molière; Harvey, the physician, before Peignet. The Würtemberger, Kepler (cotemporary with Bacon) equalled all these great men in intellect and depth of thought, for he not only ascertained the true principle of the earth's movement round the sun, but he discovered principles upon which rest many theories of modern astronomy. His calculations enabled us to discover worlds invisible to the eye, even when aided by the sharpest instruments. This was the case with Kant, who in theory saw, with his mind's eye, Uranus shining in the heavens twenty-six years before Herschel discovered it, *de facto*, with the assistance of his gigantic telescope. The Germans in deductive, and the English in inductive sciences, have always been in advance of the French.

If we enter still deeper into the difference of the results which were the consequences of the English and French Revolutions, we find that the Revolutions in England were not merely political, but also thoroughly social. Society was corrupt, government was depraved, the aristocracy licentious, the clergy stationary, the officials not to be trusted. Oaths were of no value, confidence, and all moral ties upon which rests human society, were loosened. It was necessary to create an entirely new element; the State must be restored upon a totally new foundation, with the assistance of the incorruptible, honest, and unsophisticated middle-class, and it is only since this has been the case, that England has become really free. Inequality in sight of the law ceased, the person of the lowest beggar in the State became inviolable, the king was set up as the embodiment of the supreme power in the State; his officials, as servants of the people, became responsible. Thus, notwithstanding its monarchical principle, England's constitution was founded upon a pure democratical basis, by which means its freedom was finally secured. This democracy, contented with equality of rights, did not go so far as to destroy the property of their nobles, in order to introduce, by an instrument of murder invented for the occasion, freedom and equality of possession. Legally and practically have the English abolished the exclusive privileges of the nobles, thus depriving despotism of its tools, and obliging the nobles to find their only support in the people.

But it was different in France, where everything was based upon vague theories, hollow declamation, superficial wit, and fine-sounding phrases; where principles and actions were in continual opposition; where a Rousseau could write a long and brilliant book on education,* reproaching the mothers of France with their careless indifference

* "Emile," 1762, par Jean Jacques Rousseau.

in intrusting their babies to nurses, while, according to his own shameless confessions,* he sent his children to the refuge for foundlings; so that, in spite of his high-sounding device, " Vitam impendere vero," his actions gave the lie to his theories. Voltaire pursued the same course. He scorned every religious form and creed; yet he became the most venal slave of outward court-formalities. He played the part of Frederick the Great's court-fool at the same time that he betrayed his protector to the French government; propagating on one side liberal ideas,† after having written an apotheosis on the most despicable tyrant, Louis le Grand.‡ Voltaire's frivolous and superficial writings assisted greatly throughout the Continent in sowing a spirit of levity in the most sacred questions and interests of humanity. He sacrificed virtue and truth to wit, refinement of style, and the ambiguity of startling paradoxes. To astonish and strike the mind of the people seemed to be the task of science, literature, and philosophy. A destructive State-policy, which endeavoured to annihilate that which was established,—to break down to-day what it had built yesterday,—was the

* "Confessions," par Jean Jacques Rousseau, 1760.
† "Idées Republicaines," par Voltaire, 1762.
‡ "Siècle de Louis le Grand," par Voltaire, 1752.

consequence of this mania to astonish and strike. Voltaire wished for reforms, but, by his witty levity, he destroyed in advance every faith in an honest principle of possible reform. Let us consider the third forerunner of the French Revolution, Helvetius. He, in theory, raved for every possible freedom, but practically opposed the abolition of the cruel game-laws of France, and, in this point he placed himself on a level with the most absolute tyrant.

This same spirit of contradiction is only too perceptible in all those nations who, incapable of developing themselves, took France as their guide and model for imitation. As a proof of this, I will cite only two out of the many passages in your own work that illustrate this want of principle. In page 191 of your work, you exclaim: "What a grand prospect is open to a great French statesman, who casts his eagle-glance afar! [Do you not think that we are able fully to appreciate your allusion to the eagle here?] In the grand high-road by which he may hold sway in all the southern part of Europe right to Constantinople, the only break is the broad space called Hungary. France has already, in principle, emancipated Italy, and she too was the *de facto* liberator of the

Danubian principalities. That is why France alone now has moral authority and influence in those two countries. But to pass from Italy to the Danubian Principalities all Hungary must be traversed. Well, if the same political service were rendered to that country,—and it might be effected with smaller sacrifices, for Hungary, with her 15,000,000 inhabitants, rather requires moral than material support,—the moral power of France would then resemble an electric wire, which, starting from Paris, would pass without a single interruption across Italy, Hungary, the Danubian Principalities, to Constantinople, that is, to the East, where the fate of the world will have to be decided."

I do not know how your master will be pleased by your thus divulging the plans of the great Napoleonistic conspiracy to which we have already alluded at the beginning of this letter. I will now cite the second passage in the same book, in which you offer a similar sway to England, whose institutions are diametrically opposed to every principle propagated by the despot on the other side of the Channel (p. 215). After having flattered Lórd Palmerston for his brilliant political career, *which you say belongs to history*, you call upon the

English government to help you in obtaining the same end, promising them what you have now graciously given up to France. The passage is as follows: "By our customs, our usages, our political ideas, by all that constitutes the most religious and public life of a people, the Hungarians represent English civilization in the East, just as the Poles and Romans represent French ideas. This circumstance has a most important bearing on English interests in the East."

We need make no further remark; it is sufficient only to cite these passages to hold up to contempt the utterly confused ideas which beset the imitators of French policy.

What has been the consequence in France of such a contradiction between theory and practice? A republic changed into an empire, the abolition of a God, and the adoration of a lost woman as Goddess of Reason, a freedom that punished thought with death, a police more cruel than the most cruel eastern despot. Fire, sword, desolation and murder, licentiousness in every direction, quickly followed by a centralized imperial government, a new made aristocracy, a hierarchy which reestablishes the priests in their unlimited sway over the mind and body of the people; a miserable restoration with constitutional institutions that were soon held up to mockery and of which they sought to rid themselves by ordinances. Then a "citizen-king" that swindled on the Bourse, traded in stocks, sanctioned bribery, and at last cowardly gave way to a republic whose leaders decorated themselves with the red ribbons of the *Legion d'Honneur*, and were proud of sitting on the velvet seats of the royal boxes in the theatres. A continual centralization of power, which procures government appointments for the few wordy heroes, who by their practice constantly contradict their own theories, who care only to visit operas and balls, and keep mistresses, who merely riot and carouse at the expense of the industrial classes. We cannot be astonished that such a state should send out its republican soldiers, not to assist the nations of Europe in their struggles for liberty, but to restore Papacy to Rome, to put down the Roman republic. We cannot wonder that a people, whose leaders, to whatever party they may belong, are entirely without a spirit of perseverance, at last allow themselves to be oppressed, gagged, and sent to Cayenne! And yet you expect France to deliver Europe!

I will now mention a few German thinkers,

who will indeed offer a striking contrast to those of France. They were pure, lofty, sublime and spiritual men, whose theories were at unity with their lives. I will only mention Herder, Kant, Fichte, Hegel, and Humboldt! The lives of these men, the intellectual heroes of Germany, stand pure and dazzlingly bright before the eyes of the world. They meant all they wrote, and acted accordingly. How is it that in spite of such teachers Germany has not yet been able to secure that alpha of freedom—security of the person?

We attribute this to an unnatural mania for *Frenchifying* all our institutions, our literature and society. Lessing tried to exclude the French from the Temple of German Art; and the consequence of it was that characters like Saladin, Nathan, Minna von Barnhelm, Götz von Berlichingen, Wallenstein, Tell, and Faust supplied the place of nonsensical *buffons*, by which the French represented Greek heroes in silk stockings and knee-breeches. But, in spite of all this, comedy, which still delights the Germans, remains thoroughly French; it is full of French frivolity and ambiguous plots. We were ashamed of our honest morality; we did not think our poets capable of being so brilliantly perverted as the French, who are not ashamed to lay bare the greatest vulgarity, and show a degraded nature veiled in wit with which they excuse every corruption.

But we have gone even farther! We have allowed ourselves to be so infatuated by the political theories of the French with regard to property, right of association, and the duties of the government, that we gave ourselves up to the most absurd illusions, entirely losing sight of all that was practical and possible. The most sophistical, perverted, and various theories were propagated amongst us. But happily we Germans were too much occupied with theories; we had so little decision that we seldom came to action; if however this was the case, our attempts were so restricted by every description of system, that a wholesome reaction, brought about by men who had decided principles in view, was sure to triumph everywhere to save us from all French illusions.

The whole continent was enervated by eccentric romances originating in France, calculated to excite the senses, and please the people by holding out most agreeable political systems, according to which every one would be equally rich, and without much labour would become free and powerful. Thus we have to thank the poisonous pest-breathing influence of France, which equally enslaves State and religion, for every dissension, indolent submission, moral weakness, and enervated indifference. Without any kind of fixed principles, French philosophy is tossed on the stormy waves of scepticism from one system to another, always seeking for brilliant problems, passing by what is simple, necessary, and natural; erecting a building without foundations; discussing without fixed and reasonable principles. The French in later times, have made woman the chief object of their writings, and in trying to analyse her position, they have entirely mistaken the beautiful and sublime calling of the weaker sex. They talk of the intellectual and moral development of the woman, but in reality they try to create her without morals, without shame. They are bent upon bursting off the tender bloom of innocence and gentle submission from her character, and without virtuous women a State cannot become free.

The French Government at last created a kind of centralized official State, and these officials have now degenerated into police; so that we could divide Frenchmen only into two classes, that is to say, police and non-police. The military is nothing more nor less than an armed police. The priests are the most secret allies of that same police; the State itself nothing but police. All who do not belong to the police are guarded, watched, and led by them. It ought to be the task of government to protect, without partiality, the weak from the strong, to execute the laws made by the people, to maintain the public peace, to promote commerce, to enforce sanitary measures, and to attain unlimited freedom and the highest morality by an unrestricted gradual development of the people. In a free State, to be moral, and in a moral State, to be free, is the aim the attainment of which, in theory and practice, occupies human society the more, the more it becomes conscious of its real destination. This, however, can never be effected by those means which, till now, have had full play in France.

Europe stands before the gates of a future full of threatening political convulsion. It will be the duty of England, in conjunction with Germany, to make head against the Franco-Russian schemes of conquest. Under Germany we mean Prussia in close alliance with Austria; for we think that in the coming struggle, neither England nor Prussia

will be able to spare the 90,000 men, which
Austria, in case of war, as a member of the German
Confederation, is obliged to bring into the
field. If Austria should be slighted, she will, perhaps,
be compelled, contrary to her own inclinations,
to throw herself into the arms of her most
deadly foes. England and Germany must unite
against the schemes of a State like France, where
domestic life is undermined, the commercial life
broken, and the life of the State without an organization
which can promote its natural development;
where all the fundamental pillars of a
community are wanting; where the present constitution
is but a mere form, without either roots
or vitality. Should a second Napoleon be permitted
to turn his restless hordes into the fields of
Europe, and should he call the Magyars to his
assistance, as you propose, he may find sympathy
with those revolutionary myrmidons of the movement
of 1848 who live on the alms which this
foreign despot deigns to throw to them,—trading
thus with their liberal ideas,—yet certainly not
with the masses of the Austrian people; for it
ought to be known that, in the last Italian war, the
Austrian commanders alone, by their jealousies,
and the military administration, by their defalca-

tions, were the causes of their unsuccessful campaign. The Austrian people and the Austrian soldiers were not defeated; and to prove this assertion, I will quote a passage from a pamphlet by a high military authority, which has appeared in Berlin, under the title "Savoyen Nizza und der Rhein."*

In writing about the bravery of the Austrians, he says: "No parade drilling, no red-tape service, no corporal's stick has been capable of driving out of the Germans their invincible love of fighting (Rauftalent). In spite of the tight clothing, the heavy knapsacks, these young recruits, who had never smelt powder, stood their ground like veterans against the experienced, lightly dressed and lightly armed Frenchmen, and it was only with the greatest amount of incapability and discord that the Austrian leaders made it possible that such troops were beaten. And how were they beaten? The French could boast of no trophies, no colours, hardly any cannons, and but few prisoners! The *only colour that* was taken, was found under a heap of slain, and the unwounded

---

* See an excellent critique on this pamphlet in the London German newspaper, "Hermann," No. 66, pp. 522 and 523. We can sincerely recommend this paper to any English journalist who wishes to make himself acquainted with German politics.

prisoners were Italian and Hungarian deserters.* From the private to the major, the Austrian army has covered itself with glory, and this glory belongs particularly to the German-Austrians. The Italian troops were not to be trusted, therefore most of them were sent away; the Hungarians deserted in crowds or were doubtful; the Croats fought in this campaign decidedly worse than usual; therefore, the German-Austrians may justly appropriate all the glory to themselves."

This impartial Prussian writer proves that there exist still elements in Austria, which, by a better organization, could easily be converted into an invincible power, and Germany, a second time provoked, would soon drive back the Franco-Celtic legions over the Rhine. The next war-cry which will resound in Germany against French despotism, which aspires to hold unlimited sway over State, religion, literature, and fashion will be, "Down with it for ever," and many a Frenchman will re-echo this cry.

The thinkers of Germany as well as the liberals

* To the honour of the Hungarian deserters we may mention that hunger and not treachery drove them over to the enemy; for we know from an eye witness, that in consequence of the bad administration of the commissariat, they had been forty-eight hours without food before they left the Austrian army.

of every nationality in Austria, with the exception of a few ultra-Magyars, know only too well—thanks to a free and independent press—that European civilization has nothing to hope from despotic France.

Hénault says, " Laws and manners are the soul of history." Now the French laws are despotic, French manners corrupt: who then but a short-sighted politician, or a fanatic partisan of those petty nationalities in the East, could or would hope anything from that country?

ANSWER VII.

The sad experience which Austria has had during the last ten years, must have taught the government that the old bureaucratic system is no longer capable of guiding the helm of State, without the assistance of modern opinions and principles, which have been developed gradually and almost imperceptibly. In former times Germany, in which Austria must of course be included, unfortunately derived many of her legal and political institutions from Rome as she now does from France; and that which increases the evil is that Austria especially wished to govern by means of the most corrupt measures of ancient Roman and modern French State-policy, viz., casuistry in politics, a double-tongued diplomacy in conjunction with an army of mean delators! Hoping to misrepresent public opinion, not only at home, but throughout Europe, France, under a Louis Napoleon, has established a "*Bureau de l'esprit public,*" an office which regulates the public opinion of the people, and through which alone the wants of the masses can be made known. This "*Bureau de l'esprit public*" is a kind of Inquisition, where all ideas, opinions and assertions unfavourable to the government are condemned to eternal silence. This tribunal, however, goes even further than this; it misrepresents, misleads, and stupifies the public opinion; belies the present and the future, and stifles every true and free thought before it is even expressed. Yet we find men who formerly placed themselves in the ranks of those who struggled, fought and died for liberty, actually desiring to propagate such a system. It is difficult to say how long this system, with its secret leading-article and pamphlet manufactories will be able to exist. This art of governing, under the cloak of democratical clap-trap, endeavours to agitate States and nations; but it is more than probable that this scheme will meet with a determined and successful opposition in the simple honesty of the Germans. If you, or any other of the paid Imperial revolutionists, whose machinations thinking politicians have already discovered, wish to hold up France as the deliverer of Europe, you are labouring under a great delusion, if you imagine that we are incapable of distinguishing between freedom and slavery. The French autocrat tries to make the Belgians believe that it would increase their wealth and promote trade, if they would allow their country to become a province of France. In Servia, Bulgaria, and Bosnia a federative Slave State under the Protectorship of Napoleon is talked of, and the laws and organization of this future kingdom are already mentioned. From Switzerland Germany receives promise of unity, freedom, and a 'real democracy under the liberal sway of Napoleon. On the Rhine newspapers are published, which try to prove to the German people how happy and free they would be, if they would only permit French soldiers to infest their country for a few months. The old Bonapartist proclamations of 1809 are again revived and circulated for the edification of the Magyars, to assist in the formation of a Magyar kingdom, organized on oligarchic principles. Whilst the Magyars are sounding, now the English, now the Russian court, now paying their addresses in the ante-chambers of Prince Napoleon, trying to induce some one of them to accept the Hungarian crown, or to take pity on the grand Eastern confederation; they have already drawn the future map of Europe, in which Austria and Germany no longer occupy the position of independent States, as centres of middle European commerce and trade, supported by the invincible power of German intellect. The monarchs living on the banks of the Seine and the Neva imagine that the Germans, like the Greeks, are so enervated by their philosophers, that they are unfit for the turmoil of war, and can only exist as a learned people, scattered abroad, without home, without country; driven from their native vineyards to wander about, explaining the Teutonic classics to the unintellectual inhabitants of Bosnia, Servia, and Arabia, and the miserable dwellers on the banks of the Orinoco, Ganges, or Yellow River,—to propound the Niebellungenlied to them instead of Homer; Schiller and Goethe instead of Tyrtæus and Anacreon; Johannes Müller, Rotteck, or Schlosser, instead of Thucydides; or Kant and Hegel instead of Aristotle,—to nurse little children, and establish systems. As the Greeks of old assisted Rome and the Middle Ages, the Germans are to help out the modern world with their original ideas, and spread abroad knowledge and civilization; while they themselves, however, are to exist without home and without country! It is only the French, with their valiant sword and their cunning *bureau de l'esprit public*, and the Russians, with their primitive barbarism, and their modern allies the discontented Magyars, who are to be allowed to possess the world!

But they are mistaken. The signs of the times show only too clearly that they have the presumption to attempt to make Europe Cossac. It depends entirely upon the governments themselves whether they will retain their monarchical institutions or become republics. The Prince-Regent of Prussia has chosen the only means which can avert the threatening danger. He is carrying out an open, honourable policy, that meets with sympathy throughout Germany. The Emperor of Austria, since the 19th of April, has also entered upon the path of reform.

It would be very wrong to draw comparisons between this step and the fraudulent proceeding of a Charles I. of England, or Louis XVI. of France. Let us hear what the great Macaulay describes, in a few words, as Charles's proceedings with respect to the Petition of Rights:

"The Lords and Commons present him with a bill, in which the constitutional limits of his power are marked out. He hesitates; he evades; *at last, he bargains to give his assent for five subsidies.*

The bill receives his solemn assent; the subsidies are voted; but, no sooner is the tyrant relieved, than he returns at once to all his arbitrary measures, which he had bound himself to abandon, and violates all the clauses of the very Act which he had been paid to pass."*

This bargaining, this low bartering, sealed the doom of Charles I. He gave a solemn promise, accepted payment for that promise, and then broke it. Louis Napoleon is the only man we can compare with Charles I.; he took a solemn oath to maintain the French Republic; but, as soon as he had encumbered it with debts, he betrayed it, and destroyed it out of pure gratitude.

Louis XVI. allowed himself to be made a party to conspiracies against his own country, and against the constitution he had sworn to maintain. He felt himself unfit to guide a nation who had learned to rave enthusiastically for liberty, and commit murder, but had not learned to distinguish superficial political theories from a practical administration of government which might exist without either the tyranny of the populace or that of a despot. Louis XVI.'s conduct with regard to

* "Critical and Historical Essays," by Lord Macaulay. London: Longman, Green, Longman, and Brother, 1850. Vol. I. p. 17.

the masses was full of timidity, a crime for which no people can forgive their king. He declared all the concessions made since October, 1789, to be forced, extorted and unwillingly wrung from him, and had recourse to flight. His conduct proved that he, morally speaking, had become a nonentity in the State; and from that moment Louis XVI. was morally dead to France; he was his own executioner. This cowardly act was sufficient proof of his inability to govern. As their king was morally dead, the people dared, in spite of the acknowledged inviolability of the representative of royalty, to sentence him to death. Charles I. disgraced himself by breaking his word in a purely commercial agreement. Charles I. closed a bargain, accepted payment for his concessions, and cheated his customers. It was impossible for the free merchants of England to forgive such an act. That a leader must have *courage* was the firm belief of the descendants of the Latin Franks. Louis XVI. destroyed this belief; they would have forgiven him tyranny, dishonour, breach of faith, licentiousness, and every sort of meanness, as they did his ancestor, Louis XIV.; but cowardice could only be punished by his own death and that of his wife.

But we have nothing of this description in Austria. Government is endeavouring to carry out a grand political idea; to form a free and powerful whole out of the divided and heterogeneous parts, which have remained uncivilized because of their social and political division. The Emperor himself in his Decree of the 19th of April, declares the principle of *self*-government throughout his dominions to be the foundation of his future administration. From that moment he adopted a reform in perfect harmony with the modern ideas of State-policy. If the government and people adhere firmly and honourably to this principle, Austria must and will have a future. But it is particularly necessary that the people should make themselves acquainted with the duties which self-government imposes on them. A people that has not yet learnt to be free, takes advantage of the first opportunity which freedom offers, to use the broken chains of slavery as a means of destruction, as has been the case in France. By this means a political struggle for freedom prevents industrial, intellectual, and social development.

It is only the English and German elements that have been found to possess the capability of reorganizing a State after revolutions which have commenced in the lower classes. It is only these elements that possess the power of putting an end to anarchy by enforcing law and order. We may expect to find this subduing power in the German element of Austria. Gallicism is too deeply seated in the other nationalities to allow them to learn that true freedom consists in so restricting the actions of every citizen that each citizen can live independently. The Austrian government has firmly established the principle of self-government, and has taken steps to enable it to follow out this principle. It is now the duty of the people to take advantage of the opportunity, and show themselves worthy of governing themselves. The government looks upon Austria's past as a *tabula rasa*, and lays the foundation not of a future oligarchical constitution, but of a great, powerful, united, and free industrial State,* in which every nationality will be able to maintain itself; when the State is based upon personal liberty, a judicious exploit of raw products, and a free development of all intellectual and material

---

* All the late Decrees show that this is the wish of the government. Traffic is facilitated, trade corporations abolished, the Jew is allowed the right of possessing, and the foreign tradesman is no longer asked to become a naturalized Austrian.

powers.* The Austrian administration, as based upon the Latin-French principles, has been tried and found wanting. An irresponsible, uncontrolled bureaucracy is the State's greatest enemy. Where and how will the State find this control, so necessary for its own security, as well as that of every citizen? Solely and entirely in an honest, free, and well-regulated press, which must be looked upon as the best support of self-government. Self-government and liberty of the Press are the pillars which support all truly great and powerful States; the oligarchical privileges for which you rave are not necessary to the existence of a State.

I quite agree with you in thinking that promises and half-measures would be certain ruin; but a return to the old historical rights, which the

* It is extremely unjust, when considering the position of Austria with regard to Hungary, to declare that the Austrian government, by its protestations of reform, only intends to blind the nation. It is but natural that the French press should make such assertions, but part of the English press is also guilty of this injustice. Instead of encouraging and supporting the government when it seems to perceive the worthlessness of the old system; instead of assisting it in every way to establish a free and powerful Austria, this conduct only undermines all faith in the possibility of the undertaking, by blocking up the path to reform by suspicion and mistrust. According to my opinion, this is not only unjust but unwise. Instead of the people possessing themselves of the concessions, and endeavouring to carry them out with energy and vigour, the time is wasted in miserable indecision. Instead of freely and heartily taking the government at its word, every possible obstacle is placed in its way. *Suspicion and mistrust* must of necessity lame all the energies of a government.

Magyars insist upon without taking into consideration recent events and the demands of modern times, would be even still more dangerous.

With what justice can the old constitutional Magyars lay claim to the following five points?

1. "The restitution of the ancient historical limits of Hungary."

What right have the Magyars to make such a demand, at a time when they have not only allowed a foreign enemy to attack and rob the Austrian government of a part of its dominions, but actually deserted the army of their legal sovereign to swell the ranks of the invader; at a time when the so-called liberal leaders of Hungary, living in London and Paris, are leagued with Louis Napoleon in endeavouring to prevent the free and normal development of Europe, by compelling the different governments to make continual preparations for war. It is not the wish of the Magyars to advance the cause of freedom in Austria by their alliance with Louis Napoleon; for the government, of its own freewill, has adopted many undeniable improvements,—but it is their wish to make reform as impossible as in the times of Zapolya, Bocskay, Tököly, and Rakotzy.

2. "The re-establishment of the old constitution."

That would be the complete restoration of the Oligarchy of former times, which would be a step backwards instead of forwards. Citizen and peasant are emancipated, the nobility taxed, banking and commercial establishments erected, trade freer, and the Jew is allowed the privilege of possessing. Shall we abandon all these improvements, and return to the lawless, unprotected condition of the working-classes, for the privilege of hearing Parliamentary deputies discuss peaceful laws in braided coats and broadswords? Hungary has paid too dearly for this privilege by a complete demoralization and loosening of all social and political ties. The historical right, upon which alone this privilege was based, must give place to the demands of modern times.

Equal dangers in war, equal joys in peace, the same victories and losses, ought long ago to have united the various fractions of the different nationalities in Austria. Should the bond of union be strengthened by self-government,—which according to the Emperor's promise, is to be introduced in every province,—should commercial relations on the principles of free-trade,—should equality of right and law, as recently laid down in principle, be practised with energy,—should the government keep to uniform tenets in the administration of the whole empire,—we would soon perceive the development of a certain feeling among all the nationalities, that the welfare and misfortune of the whole is the welfare and misfortune of every individual. The central power, in advocating such principles, would create a firm bond of union in all the heterogeneous parts, and thus transform Austria into a united State, which would find its power and greatness in the equal freedom of all its citizens.

The Magyars have neither the power nor the wish to reach such an elevation in State-policy. Their past deprives them of the power, and the deeds, writings, and tendencies of their present leaders prove only too clearly that they have not even the wish to do so. The old history of the Magyars resulted in nothing; and shall this history, after having advanced socially for ten years, recommence where it left off in 1848? Such a continuation would not assist Austria, nor yet make Hungary free, and it would be an invincible obstacle to the progress of civilization.

3. "The restoration of her municipal autonomy."

This has now to take place, and upon a much

more liberal footing than formerly. In future the right of electing or being elected is not to be an exclusive privilege of the nobles, but a census is to be introduced, and anyone can be elected who possesses the talent and an ardent desire to undertake the difficult and responsible office of representative of the people. It is clearly owing to this circumstance that the Magyars have not received this law with joyful sympathy. The nobles look upon the levelling German element of the government with unfavourable eyes; they see themselves deprived by it of their oligarchical privileges. The industry of the German citizen, the trading spirit of the Servian, and the activity and perseverance of the Sclavonians, will soon enable these nationalities to become the superiors of the indolent Magyars;* and to prevent this they prefer throwing themselves into the arms of the French and Italians; and they, in good time, will give

* I will here relate an anecdote of Count Széchényi, which in its way is extremely characteristic. The celebrated Count was once haranguing his countrymen in a club, upon their national faults; he bitterly attacked their laziness and indolence, and held up England as an example for them to imitate. Carried away by his recollections of that free and industrial State, he exclaimed: "Every one works in England; lord and servant, lady and housemaid,—nothing but work, work, work!" "Then indeed I must confess that I pity the poor English from the very bottom of my heart, and am proud to think that I am not an Englishman," replied a stiffnecked Magyar.

them up to the Czar, who will convert their country into a Russian province. The love of rule, and blind pride of the oligarchs prepare a fearful future for Hungary.

4. "The re-acknowledgment of all the laws and treaties which secured the political and national independence of the kingdom."

This clause lays bare the short-sighted narrow-mindedness of the Magyars, who only care for the safety of their own political and *national* independence. The oppression of 9,000,000 people speaking other tongues is included in this political and national independence of the Magyars. It may possibly be to the interest of a despot like Louis Napoleon to support such principles for a short time; but we must condemn them when we recollect that every nationality has an equal right to develop itself according to its capabilities. In Austria the question of nationality must give way to political, commercial, and industrial questions. The more freedom Austria allows for self-development, the less she must allow nationality and religion to intermeddle with politics. On the lovely banks of the Danube, as on the shores of the smiling Rhine, a vigorous, productive, creative, labouring, and acquiring State will and must

ANSWER VII. 215

rise out of a firmly-established liberty. The old ideas of State-policy, with their constitutional forms wanting in internal stability, allowing small as well as large States to do as they like, mutually counteracting each other's development, and bringing about the causes described in these pages, are corrupt and decayed; they have fallen from the ever fresh and vigorous tree of time. The rotten branch of bureaucracy, severed from the parent-stem by fraud and suicide, has fallen even with a still more fearful crash. It would be dreadful if Austria's government and nation were to pass by this phenomenon heedlessly.

It is only where social and political matters require a thorough reform, that symptoms of extraordinary maladies are perceptible in the body of the State. Statistics and political economy, with their regular and astonishing returns of numbers always at certain times and under certain circumstances, show often too powerfully where the evil lies. The increase of suicide in Austria shows that the disorganization in the State increases. The number of suicides is much greater in countries where the government is despotic, than where a liberal administration is at the head of a nation. The number of suicides in France, Prussia and Russia,* is much greater than in England. In Austria, the greatest number of suicides used to be committed by soldiers, and now a frightful number have been committed amongst the government officials.

Love, misery, self-caused or chronic diseases, and debauchery, are, generally speaking, the causes of suicide; but suicide committed because of fraudulent conduct towards the government is an evil which requires a speedy remedy. The word which can effect this improvement has been spoken by the Emperor himself: that word is *self-government*, not merely self-government for the Magyars, founded upon Magyar exclusive principles, but self-government for every community in every district and comitat of the great empire,—self-government for the whole of Austria. The consequences of a free, regulated self-government in Austria will be that the arts and sciences, finances, trade, commerce, and riches of the country will develop themselves with extraordinary rapidity. By a free administration, the individual is ele-

* The number of suicides in Petersburg, amounted in 1810, to 94; in 1822, to 986; in 1823, to 1069; in 1824, to 1066; in 1825, to 966; in 1826, 1176; and they are gradually but constantly increasing. See Malhen, Bibliohek der Welt-Kunde, 1830, p. 213.

vated, and "the worth of a State, in the long run, is the worth of the individuals composing it." Under the former circumstances, Austria could not commence the intellectual and moral expansion and elevation of her citizens with sufficient energy. The best and only remedy is self-government. Austria herself wishes it; she no longer aspires to be governed by an artificial administrative State-machine, by which means." a State dwarfs its men in order that they may be more docile instruments in its hands, even for beneficial purposes."

Austria has made the sad experience that with small men no great thing can really be accomplished, and that the perfection of machinery, to which it has sacrificed everything, will in the end avail it nothing for want of the vital power which, in order that the machine might work smoothly, it has, till now, preferred to banish. But the principle of self-government puts an end to this, and brings vitality into the State, and with vitality, energetic activity, commerce, trade, and mutual confidence will be restored, and the state of the finances improved; for the administration of the communities, and the management of the rural and local police will fall to the share of the communities themselves, and the administration will be better attended to than now, if committed to the unpaid care of the cleverest members of the community. Thus the State will be rid of the heavy burden of supporting a numerous army of lazy officials, who drain the national coffers without bringing in the slightest return. It would be easy for Austria to introduce such a reform; it would only be necessary for the government to superannuate the employés now in office, and immediately begin to organize the communities. The budget would then have the prospect of being delivered in time from an oppressive burden in this branch of the administration, and an increase of strength in the Austrian government would be the consequence. On the other side it is necessary for every citizen to make himself acquainted with his duties. This will be Austria's greatest difficulty. The people will only learn by degrees not to expect everything from the government. It is this mistaken idea that prevails in France, and sustains the spirit of protection. The people must begin by thinking and acting for themselves, seeking only their own advancement by promoting the general welfare.

It will be the duty of the State to see that the

laws are everywhere observed. In a State based upon the principle of self-government, the people will not think of feeding insolent officials. Instead of officials the citizens will undertake the duties of administration themselves. The citizen who neglects these duties must be punished with the utmost rigour of the law; for if a citizen expects rights and privileges from a State, he must undertake duties towards that State. If a State places its laws and institutions on a liberal footing, in order to insure the performance of these duties, it throws all responsibilities on to the shoulders of the citizens, and must enforce obedience to the laws. The majesty of principle and law takes possession of its rights, hitherto usurped by despotism, and whilst the citizen is the lawgiver, the government becomes the executive power.

The difference of the education and capabilities of the various nationalities will oblige Austria to pay great attention to the manners, customs, and even languages, of all the tribes who acknowledge her sway; but she must never be induced to give up the political autonomy of the central power by creating separate kingdoms. The different nationalities may 'develop themselves locally and socially as they please; but the laws they must one and all receive from a free central Parliament consisting of two houses, or else Austria will fall to pieces, and become a Russian province. Hungary must be considered only as an integral part of free Austria, and must give up the dream of possessing a constitution based upon the old oligarchical principles, which would prevent the progress of the spirit of the times. The Irish, notwithstanding their difference of religion, their origin, and isolated position, have been obliged to form an integral part of Great Britain, and they have no reason to complain of their position. During the long years of her rule over Hungary, Austria has never been so hard upon the Magyars as the free constitutional Governments, *i.e.*, Parliaments and kings, of England have been upon Ireland. But this harshness has not been without beneficial results Agriculture and trade have improved, and wealth increased in Ireland. Ireland has given England immortal warriors, statesmen, and poets, who, without the more extensive sphere of action afforded them by the mother country, would have died in the lovely Emerald Isle, unhonoured and unknown. If every citizen of Austria begins to feel proud of belonging to a great empire, he will soon see his own liberty and welfare promoted in it.

5. "Lastly, the maintenance of the Pragmatic Sanction, that is to say, dynastic union with the Austrian provinces, but only on condition that they shall have a constitution."

The Austrian people must, I am sure, feel deeply grateful for such kind interest. But, unfortunately you betray the want of sincerity concealed in this wish. In page 191, etc., you offer Hungary to France, and in page 215 you offer it to England; which conduct is, of course, quite compatible with your wish for the dynastic union with the Austrian Provinces. The hackneyed phraseology of Magyar Statesmen is really pitiable. They repeat the same thing over and over again; they are continually grumbling, without being able to tell what it is they are grumbling about; continually talking, but never acting; always isolating themselves, yet wishing to keep pace with the rest of Europe; thinking meanly, but talking grandly; acting corruptly, but wishing to be judged favourably; prating about liberty, yet treating everyone despotically but themselves; organizing States, yet incapable of managing their own houses; severing the ties which bind them to humanity, and then complaining that they are left without support!*

The Magyars must rouse themselves, and acknowledge that the whole of their past has effected nothing for the benefit of society, either in intellect or industry; that their old reminiscences only unfit them for the future; that to attempt to roll the stone of Magyar supremacy to the top of the mountain is as useless as the work of Sisyphus; for the more the States round Hungary acquire political unity, the faster the Magyar supremacy falls to the ground.

Neither England nor Germany will calmly look on while Austria is dismembered, for that would be promoting the Franco-Russian universal despotism. Louis Napoleon wishes to humble Prussia

---

* When Magyar citizens, who are called to the council tables, refuse to take part in the deliberations for the benefit of the whole of Austria, they show themselves incapable of enjoying political privileges. Whoever refuses to fulfil a political duty, declares himself unworthy of his rights. In the refusal of the Magyars, belonging to the national party, to take part in the consultations for the organization of the united empire of Austria, we see nothing more than a fresh proof of their incorrigibly exclusive tendencies, and their concealed hypocrisy, in pretending to wish for the constitutional development of the empire, when in reality they do everything to prevent it. But neither the Austrian people nor the Austrian government are to be frightened from the right path by such means as this. The Magyar aristocratic party will be obliged to accept what is necessary for the harmonious existence of a powerful Austria, and what at last will be carried out without their assistance.

as he humbled Austria for having refused him the hand of the Princess Vasa, declined to give up the ashes of the Duke of Reichstadt, and prevented the Pope going to Paris to adorn the "nephew of his uncle" with the French crown. Therefore, Louis Napoleon conspires with Russians, Magyars, Bulgarians, Bosnians, and Servians, hoping by these means to engage Austria at home, that he may rob Prussia more conveniently of the Rhine provinces. In the midst of peace the despot of France burdens all Europe with the expenses of a war-establishment, and compels the different nations to employ their finances in preparing for the defence of themselves and each other from the ambitious schemes of conquest of a Louis Napoleon; in whose golden snares languish the champions of Magyar freedom.*

England, as well as Germany and Austria, will be obliged to oppose, with all its power, the conspiracy against civilization which emanates from

* While sending our last proof to the printer we have been surprised by a new imperial pamphlet from Paris, under the title: "La Rupture de l'Alliance Anglaise; est elle possible?" By this work all our misgivings are perfectly justified. England and Germany are treated with the greatest insolence as third and fourth rate powers, and the author points to Russia as the only possible and sincere ally of France, with whose help the Imperial Autocrat hopes to reorganise Europe and to establish the French dominion over the world!

the Tuileries. To-day it was Nizza and Savoy, to-morrow it will be Naples, and the next day Belgium will be united with France; then the dominions on the Rhine will be extended, and, at last, the road through Italy and Hungary to Constantinople and the Black Sea, will be occupied. England's trade with the Mediterranean, Adriatic, and the Black Seas, will be cut off, her dominion in India threatened by the completion of the Suez Canal; Germany will be bound hand and foot; Austria dismembered. Instead of Turkey, small States, under Russian rule, will lift their heads on the Danube. And it is to this Franco-Russian universal despotism, which will trample on the civilization and progress of the world, that the Magyars, Bulgarians, and Bosnians, bow in blind adoration, promising, with its assistance, to establish Europe's future freedom.

The conspiracy is only too visible; it is no longer a secret. England is armed to the teeth, Prussia prepares for war, Austria is on the *qui vive.* The only thing that is to be wondered at is, that each seems reluctant to be the first to strike the inevitable blow. But the longer the struggle is postponed, the more fierce and bloody it will be. We need not fear for Europe's future: Germany's sword, England's energy, and Austria's caution, will deliver Europe yet once again, and we hope for ever, from the restless spirit of a French despot, and the trivial quarrels of nationalities.

THE END.

INDEX.

ANSWER I.

	PAGE
INTRODUCTION	1
Statistical remarks on the different Races in Hungary	3
Count Stephen Széchényi	4
Flattery does not improve a nation	5
Position of the Author	8
Spirit of the Hungarian Constitution	9
The "*misera plebs contribuens*"	11
Egypt, India, and Peru, compared with Hungary	13
Political Liberty—an exclusive privilege of the Magyars	15
The disaster at Mohacs	18
England under Charles II.	21
Buckle on the history of every civilized nation	22

ANSWER II.

Government and their influence upon a nation	24
The Germans and the Reformation	25
The voice of truth	26
Consequences of the Magyar dominion in general	28
The cause of the evil	30

	PAGE
What has the Magyar constitution done for the Citizen and the Peasant	31
The Magnates and their social position	ib.
The Roman Catholic Clergy	37
The Nobility	39
The Sandal-nobility (Bocskoros)	42
The Burghers	46
The Peasant	48
More lawyers than burghers and peasants	50

ANSWER III.

Hungary from a religious point of view	52
Tolerance in Hungary	53
Casuistry in politics	54
John Zapolya	55
Queen Mary and Luther	57
Decision of the Magnates against the Lutherans	58
Zapolya's alliance with the Turks	59
60,000 Christians carried into slavery	61
Ferdinand I. and the Protestant preacher, Devay	63
Education of the Emperor-King	65
Maximilian I.	66
Maximilian and his ideas of reform	67
Maximilian and Martin Eisengrün	69
Rudolph, his education, character, and occupations	ib.
Bishop Bornemissza	71
Draskovitch made Cardinal	72
Matthias	74
Archbishop Forgács	75
Cardinal Peter Pazman	ib.

	PAGE
The Germans are victorious at the end of the Thirty-years' War.—The reason of it	76
Ferdinand II.	77
Count Stephen Palfy	78
Nicolaus Eszterhazy and Adam Thurzo	79
Ferdinand III.	80
The Romish clergy after the Peace of Linz	81
Leopold I. and Maria Theresia	83
Franz Nádasdy, Chief Justice of Hungary	84
The monarchical form of government	85
Why is England superior to Wales and Ireland	87
Joseph II.	88
The spirit of progress in Austria	89
Mill "On Liberty"	90

ANSWER IV.

There is nothing accidental in the development of a nation	92
The "Magyars the bulwark of Christendom"	93—94
John Zapolya	94
Bocskay	ib.
Fessler on Sigismund Rakotzy	96
Tendencies of the Liberals	97
German boys sent to the Turks	99
Bocskay poisoned	101
Gabriel Bethlen and George Rakotzy	102
The Germans delivering Hungary from the Turks, and Emerich Tököly	104
Leopold and Caraffa	105
England and Scotland united	106
Francis Rakotzy	107
His Memoirs	108

	PAGE
On the people	110
On the rebellious troops	111
Views on the sanctity of an oath	112
How Bocskay became a rebel	115
About the peasants	117
Rakotzy on Count Berzsenyi	118
Philosophers precede every great political movement	120

ANSWER V.

Austria humbled the aristocracy	123
Gunpowder and its influence	124
Equal taxation	126
Adam Smith's Four General Maxims on Taxation	127
The "Westminster Review" on Hungary	131
Probable influence of equal taxation	133
Difficulties to be overcome by Austria	134
The administration of justice improved	135
Tolerance and intolerance	139
Right of the Magyars to introduce their language	141
German the only possible official language	144
Statistical remarks on Newspapers	145
Germanism and criticism	146
Effects of criticism	147
Great States striving for union	148
Austria and the Nationalities	150
Relation of the Magyars to the Germans	151
Austria and the trade corporations	155
Consequences of the former trade regulations	156
The future of the Austrian Empire	158
Plato and the modern Statesmen	160
Intellect the only fit guide of a State	161

ANSWER VI.

	PAGE
Louis Napoleon and the Magyars	163
Louis XIV. and Louis Napoléon	165
The Restoration of an Occidental Empire	167
French Policy and Influence	169
Influences on the development of National Character	171
France and the French	174
Maurice of Saxony and his love	175
The people in France	177
The English Language and the French Revolutionary Heroes	178
Consequences of the French Revolutions	179
Causes of England's Success in her Revolutionary Movements	181
Industry and its Influence on the Development of a State	183
England always preceded France in her great intellectual and social movements	184
Theories in continual opposition with actions in France	186
Rousseau, Voltaire, Helvétius	187
The Magyars and the French	188
The Magyars and the English	189
Consequences of contradiction between theory and practice	190
German thinkers	191
French ideas on the Continent	193
France and her centralized official state	194
Europe and the Franco-Russian schemes	195
The Austrians and the last war in Italia	197
Hénault on the soul of history	199

ANSWER VII.

Austria and France	200
The art of governing as practised by Louis Napoléon	201
The Franco-Russian plans against Germany	203

	PAGE
Europo—Cossac	204
Charles I.	ib.
Louis XVI.	205
Austria and self-government	207
How to develop Austria's resources	208
The Magyars and their claims	210
The actual State of Europe	222
Conclusion	224

www.ingramcontent.com/pod-product-compliance
Lightning Source LLC
Chambersburg PA
CBHW031744230426
43669CB00007B/474